DWELL IN
THE WORD

DWELL IN THE WORD

A Study for College Students in Christian Community

Lucas A. Newton

ISBN: 9781096894544

"Let the word of Christ dwell in you richly…"

Colossians 3:16

TABLE OF
CONTENTS

INTRODUCTION

This study is written to encourage you to better know Jesus Christ through his word and by his Spirit. As you behold Jesus you will also learn more about yourself as you are transformed more and more into his image.

There are studies for eleven weeks in this book. They are intended to be meaningful whether you invest ten minutes a week or ten minutes everyday for a week on each lesson. If you only spend a few minutes in each lesson, I encourage you to prioritize the Scripture passages listed at the start of each chapter. Following those passages is a set of questions to help you reflect on what you have read. There is an additional section "For Further Study" that you may want to check out if that week's topic interests you.

You may notice that four of the seven initial questions in each chapter are repeated each week:

> 1. *What stands out to you in these passages?*
>
> 5. *How do these passages testify to Christ?*
>
> 6. *What does this passage mean for you as one who is in Christ?*
>
> 7. *What are you going to do in response? Who can you get to help you?*

The first question is intended to help you reflect on the Scripture that you have just read. Please do not feel pressure to try to answer the question in a certain way that you think I may want it to be answered. The Spirit wants to speak to you through the Word of God. It is important to take time and listen. This first question is meant to give you space to slow down and reflect on what the Lord is saying to you.

The fifth question is based off a belief that all of Scripture points to Jesus in some way or another. There will be more discussion about why this is so in chapter three, but it is worth it to start thinking about Scripture in view of Christ even prior to chapter three. If this question is difficult for you to answer, I encourage you to talk to other believers about it. There is a lot of benefit in talking to others about Scripture and we do well to wrestle with its meaning together.

The sixth question is an application question. It acknowledges that Scripture is about Jesus and frames the question in light of the reality that you, as a believer, are *in* Jesus. This question is intended to keep application tied to the meaning of the text and to encourage you to keep it in its canonical context. There will be more on this in chapter three, but go ahead and start trying to think through the application of Scripture in this way.

Finally, the seventh question is meant to give you an opportunity make a plan of action in light of the Scriptures you have read. We do not want to be people who engage the Word of God and walk away from the experience unchanged. This question is intended to help you focus on action steps and how you can engage others in the process. Do not be shy about sharing these steps with other believers and asking them to encourage you towards obedience.

1. THE GOSPEL

"Now after John was arrested, Jesus came into Galilee,
*proclaiming the **gospel** of God,*
and saying, 'The time is fulfilled, and the kingdom of God is
at hand;
*repent and believe in the **gospel**."*
Mark 1:14-15

Knowing and believing the Gospel changes everything. When we believe the Gospel, we place our faith and trust in Jesus and he gives us his Spirit. The Spirit works within us making us new and conforming us more and more into the image of Jesus according to the Father's will.

We are also called to share the Gospel with others. If you know the Gospel well enough to believe it, you know it well enough to share it! It is important that we never force someone to make a decision to follow Jesus, but we do want to give others in our life every opportunity to understand, believe, and obey the Gospel.

Finally, we proclaim the Gospel not only to the lost, but also to each other and to ourselves in order that we may grow more in Christ.

Pray & Read: Mark 1:14-15; Romans 1:1-6; 1 Corinthians 15:1-4

1. What stands out to you in these passages?

2. Based off of these passages, how would you define the Gospel?

3. How do these passages connect the Gospel to the Old Testament? What implications do these connections carry for how we read the Old Testament?

4. According to these passages, when exactly does receiving the Gospel save you?

5. How do these passages testify to Christ?

6. What does this passage mean for you as one who is *in Christ?*

7. What are you going to do in response? Who can you get to help you?

FOR FURTHER STUDY

Something to Read

Let's focus in on two verses: 1 Corinthians 15:3-4. We are going to take our time on these two verses and walk through them phrase by phrase. The Corinthian church was confused about the significance of the resurrection and these two verses are a part of Paul's argument laying out why the resurrection is significant for our life and faith. These two verses constitute what many people believe to be an early Christian confession of faith that reflect a summary of the Gospel that Paul preached to the Corinthians.[1] If you have not memorized 1 Corinthians 15:3-4, you should do it! You would be joining a long tradition of believers that hold it fast in their hearts as a succinct confession of our faith.

"For I delivered to you as of first importance what I also received."

Paul is reminding his audience that this message is nothing new and certainly nothing insignificant. They have already heard, as have we, the Gospel and are aware that it was something of "first importance." The message was passed along, or delivered, and received. Paul is speaking this Gospel message once again to the Corinthians for the sake of clarity and to re-affirm the foundation upon which the Christian faith is built.

---

[1] John F. Walvoord and Roy B. Zuck, eds. *The Bible Knowledge Commentary: New Testament* (Colorado Springs, CO: Victor, 2000), 542.

Every component of 1 Corinthians 15:3-4 is essential. If you miss any part of it you will likely end up with a defective gospel. If you believe a defective Gospel you probably believe in a defective savior and if you have a defective savior you have a defective salvation. We want to get the Gospel right. Sometimes we are too loose, or vague, in our evangelism;[2] especially when we reduce it to "do you believe in Jesus?" or "have you invited Jesus into your heart?" Those questions are fine, but they need to be a part of a larger understanding of what those questions mean. It is important that we are speaking with clarity and are identifying the Jesus of the Gospel that was delivered to us by the apostles as a word of first importance.

Imagine talking to someone for the first time and you happen to mention my name and they exclaim, "I know Lucas A. Newton!" At that point you would recognize that you might have a mutual friend and have at least a little something in common with your new acquaintance. But suppose your new friend says, "yeah, he's such an amazing athlete and it's particularly remarkable given how short he is! Not to mention he has the most amazingly glorious head of hair!" At this point, you would realize that you are not both talking about the same Lucas A. Newton. All of your assumptions about what your acquaintance knows about me and who I am are now out the door. This same thing happens with Jesus all the time and the consequences can be much more serious. When we talk with others about Jesus and the Gospel, we need to do so seeking to make known the Jesus of the Gospel.[3]

---

[2] Evangelism is sharing the Gospel in order that others may believe and also be saved.

[3] In college I asked the technician that was installing my internet if he knew Jesus. He replied yes and we talked for a while about faith. I would have made the connection that he was Muslim much

"that Christ died for our sins"

It is *Christ* that died for our sins. Not just anyone, but the *Christ*. Christ is not a last name but a technical term meaning the promised, anointed one. You may be familiar with its Hebrew equivalent 'Messiah.' There is a whole history of God's promises about one who would come and make things right. The Old Testament reveals more and more about what the Christ would do and what kind of person he would be. People who were paying attention to God's promises were looking for this promised one to varying degrees.[4] Paul is telling us that the Christ, the chosen and promised one, has come. He fulfills all those promises and is not *only* a good man, a good teacher, a good prophet – he was and is the Christ.

The statement that he "died for our sins" reminds us that we have sinned. We must not forget that, apart from Christ, we have a problem with sin. Consider what Scripture tells us about our condition as sinners:[5]

- Brought forth in iniquity (Psalm 51:5)

- Constantly wicked and evil (Genesis 6:5; Jeremiah 17:9)

- Nobody does good (Psalm 14:3; Romans 3:10-18)

- Dead in trespasses and sins (Ephesians 2:1)

---

sooner if I had asked him if he believed in Jesus as revealed through the Bible.
[4] Luke 1:25-35; 24:21; John 1:43-51.
[5] The bulk of this list came from my former theology professor Dr. Peter Schemm.

- Children of wrath (Ephesians 2:1-3)

- Alienated from God and hostile towards him (Colossians 1:21; Ephesians 4:18)

- Guilty and Condemned (Romans 5:16-18)

- Enslaved by sin and Satan (Romans 6:17; Romans 7:5; 2 Timothy 2:26)

- Facing God's contempt (Daniel 12:2)

- Preparing to perish (Psalm 1:6; John 8:24; 2 Thessalonians 1:6-9)

- Deserving a coming judgment (John 5:28-29)

Sin is a terrible condition and it is not popular to talk about. Consider this from Richard Dawkins as an example of how the Christian idea of sin can be received:

The sin of Adam and Eve is though to have passed down the male line – transmitted through the semen according to Augustine. What kind of ethical philosophy is it that condemns every child, even before it is born to inherit the sin of a remote ancestor? …Augustine's pronouncements and debates epitomize, for me, the unhealthy preoccupation of early Christian theologians with sin. They could have devoted their pages and their sermons to extolling the sky splashed with stars, or mountains and green forests, seas and dawn choruses. These are occasionally mentioned, but the Christian focus is overwhelmingly on sin sin sin sin

sin sin sin sin. What a nasty preoccupation to have dominating your life.[6]

John Locke and Jean-Jacques Rousseau have influenced our culture, as many people still want to believe that man is basically good but is corrupted by his surroundings. However, even if one argues that we are corrupted from without and not from within, why is the outside so corrupt? It is people that mess it up! People know that the world is messed up.[7] If you read the poets and listen to the storytellers you have an excellent cultural commentary about the presence of sin in our messed up and broken world.[8]

Sometimes we soften our talk of sin by talking of brokenness. I do this often and there is an appropriate place for speaking of brokenness. The consequences of sin result in a broken people and a broken world. However, we need to be careful that we do not get away from the responsibility that we share in that brokenness.[9] We are the ones doing the breaking and we cannot overlook that in our conception of the world as broken.

Likewise, we often speak about hating the sin and loving the sinner. This can be a Christ-honoring reflection of the love God has for the world.[10] However,

---

[6] Richard Dawkins, *The God Delusion* (NY: Houghton Mifflin Company, 2006), 252-252.
[7] Deep down they know the truth. Everyone does, they just suppress it: Romans 1:18.
[8] Obviously I do not know when you are reading this, but I am fairly certain that if you were to pull up a list of the current top-40 songs you would see a lot of commentaries on things not going the way people want.
[9] Jared C. Wilson, "We are truly victims of sin, but we're also the perpetrators. We don't just suffer evil; we produce it. We *are* it." Jared C. Wilson, *Gospel Deeps* (Wheaton, IL: Crossway 2012), 101.
[10] Consider John 3:16-17 and Ezekiel 18:23; 33:11. And read just about anywhere in the Gospels for many more examples!

we should not neglect that the sinner identifies himself with the hated sin – that is what it is to be a sinner. The Bible often identifies sinners by the sin that they commit – murderers, liars, adulterers, etc. So let us be careful that in an effort to make a point – that we are to demonstrate Christ-like love – we do not remove the sense of responsibility that connects a man to his sin. Furthermore, when we see how closely man is connected to his rebellion, we see even more the depths of God's love that he would still love a sinner.

Let's take a closer look at sin and what it means. It is the condition in which we find ourselves. It is the reason that we need a Savior and need the Christ. St. Anselm of Canterbury provides a fantastic explanation of the problem we have in his *Cur Deus Homo*.[11] He notes that God demands a life fully submitted to his will.[12] To sin even once is to fail to fully submit oneself to God's will and to rob God of that which is his: a life fully submitted to him. If anyone thinks that God can simply forgive us they do not understand the magnitude of sin. It may be a finite sin, but it is against

---

[11] You can pretty easily find this online and it is worth the read. Anselm is answering the question of "why the God-Man?" (Latin: *cur deus homo*). His approach to showing why we need Jesus is similar to showing the look of a puzzle piece by placing all other pieces together of the puzzle. Even though the final piece of the puzzle is not in place you know exactly what shape and form that piece will have even without seeing it. Anselm masterfully creates a picture in which it is only made complete and satisfied with one who looks like Jesus. Thus, when you see Jesus, you realize he is the only one that could fill the empty space.

[12] St. Augustine similarly states, "So that when I now asked what is iniquity, I realized that it was not substance but a swerving of the will which is turned towards lower things and away from you." Augustine, *Confessions*, trans F. J. Sheed (Indianapolis, IN: Hackett Publishing, 2006), 132. For you C. S. Lewis lovers out there, you may recognize similar language in Lewis's essay "First and Second Things."

an infinite God.[13] It is incompatible with God's just[14] nature to not punish sin. As Anselm states, "If it is not becoming to God to do anything unjustly or irregularly, it is not within the scope of his liberty or kindness or will to let go unpunished the sinner who does not repay to God that he has taken away."[15]

So man has a problem: "man the sinner owes God, on account of sin, what he cannot repay, and unless he repays it he cannot be saved."[16] Even if a man were capable of preventing himself from committing any *further* sins, thus living his life perfectly submitted to God's will for the rest of his life, he would still have failed to live *a life* completely submitted to God's will.[17] Man is not capable of measuring up or saving himself – he has "fallen short of the glory of God."[18]

Now God is capable of living perfectly, but God is not the one who owes the debt; man is. Man owes the debt, but is incapable of it. That's the problem sin has made. As Anselm puts it, "there is no one…who can make the satisfaction except for God himself….but no one ought to make it except man; otherwise man does not make

---

[13] My friend Andrew Hopper shares this helpful illustration: If you kick a rock, nobody cares. If you kick a fish, some people might care. If you kick a dog, you've got a lot more people caring now. If you kick a cat, you are probably back to nobody caring (jk). If you kick a baby, now we have a big problem. You kick your grandma, that's really bad! You go over to England and kick the queen, dude, you deserve major punishment. The action is the same in every instance, but the level of punishment corresponds to the person against whom the action was committed against. When we speak of sin we are talking about 'kicking' and crucifying God himself.

[14] 'Just,' as in, doing the right thing.

[15] Anselm, *Cur Deus Homo*, i.xii.

[16] Ibid., i.xxv.

[17] And who among us expects to not sin again sometime before death?

[18] Romans 3:23.

satisfaction."[19] Therefore, "it is necessary that one who is God-man should make [satisfaction of God's wrath]…It is needful that the very same Person who is to make the satisfaction be perfect God and perfect man, since no one can do it except one who is truly God, and on one ought to do it except one who is truly man."[20] Jesus, the Christ, is the God-man who came on behalf of our sin to pay the debt we owed but could not pay.

He "died for" our sin on our behalf. His death was an atoning death and a propitiation for our sins.[21] His death appeases the wrath of God and provides forgiveness for man.[22] His death can, among many other things,[23] be understood as penal substitution.[24] It was 'penal' in that he was paying a penalty and 'substitutionary' in that he did it for us in our place.

Note that Paul says *our* sins." Jesus died for us. It was not for his own sins. Paul, in 1 Corinthians 15, is

---

[19] Anselm, *Cur Deus Homo,* ii.vi

[20] Ibid., ii.vi-ii.vii

[21] I include this word to expand your theological vocabulary. There has actually been a good bit of debate revolving around the translation of the word 'ιλασμος " (used in Romans 3:25; Hebrews 2:17; 1 John 2:2) as either 'expiation' (NIV) or 'propitiation' (ESV, NASB). I like 'propitiation' and believe it is consistent with teaching we see throughout Scripture. 'Expiation' is also fine too. Much wiser and better-trained godly theologians are satisfied with expiation.

[22] Romans 3:25; 1 John 2:2; 4:10.

[23] There has been a lot of discussion in the previous few decades of whether or not this is the main thing that Christ accomplished for us. It is a discussion worth having as we see that Scripture speaks of many different things happen on account of the cross. In 1 Corinthians 15 we see a good example of the substitutionary aspect of the work of Christ.

[24] Let's keep expanding that theological vocabulary. Yeah, I know what you are thinking. "Hey, 'penal' sure sounds a lot like 'penalty. I bet this term has a lot to do with the *penalty* of sin…" Yes, that is true!

assuming the sinlessness of Jesus. If he was not sinless then he would not have been dying for our sins he would have been dying for his sins.

"in accordance with the Scriptures"

The death of Christ was no afterthought or "Plan B." It is according to the plan laid out in the Scriptures. Paul is likely pointing to the Old Testament witness regarding the promised one.[25] The Old Testament is full of references to the (surprising – and difficult to understand at the time) death of the Christ. Consider Isaiah 53:5, "But he was wounded for our transgressions; he was crushed for our iniquities; upon him was the chastisement that brought us peace, and with his stripes we are healed."[26] The death of Jesus was planned.[27]

"that he was buried"

What do you bury? A body. What is the normal condition of a buried body? It is dead. What is the condition of the buried body after there days even if it was not initially dead? It becomes dead.

"that he was raised on the third day in accordance with the Scriptures"

---

[25] 1 Corinthians is generally thought to have been written at an early date. It is possible that copies of Mark may have already been in circulation among the churches, but it is unlikely that these letters would have been what Paul had in mind here. He is speaking of the portion of Scripture that we now know as the Old Testament

[26] See also Psalm 22:16; Zechariah 2:10.

[27] Other places in the New Testament affirm this: John 19:36; 1 Peter 1:18-20.

13

If Jesus is not raised there is no hope for us. If the one who set out to conquer sin and its consequences, who sought to appease God and remove the punishment of sin, has not triumphed what hope can there be? The answer is 'none' but he is raised! He is resurrected![28] He was raised by the Father as a demonstration of his approval and acceptance of Christ's sacrifice and as a demonstration that Jesus is the Christ that he says he is.[29]

Again we see that this was a part of the plan. It is a little harder to see where the resurrection was foretold in the Old Testament, but we can pick up on some implications towards it in Psalm 16:10 and Isaiah 53:8-10. Surprisingly, Jonah in the whale for three days in Jonah 1:17 is a prophetic foretelling of what would happen to Christ. I realize this sounds like a stretch,

---

[28] I put an exclamation point here because I was thrilled with the excitement and joy that accompanies such reflection on the glories of the resurrection. However, when I put the exclamation point there I was immediately disappointed with it. That line over a dot does not do justice to the emotion that I feel. Thus, I now hate the inadequacies of the exclamation point. I do not hate the exclamation point itself. It did all it could. We live in a fallen world that is full of disappointments and inadequacies. The exclamation point is just another one of them. Perhaps in the new created order exclamation points will not have such shortcomings! This might seem like another one of those ridiculous footnotes that ultimately feels like a waste of your time, but I am actually serious. What will be the depth of the redemption we will experience in the new heavens and new earth? I can only imagine. (I nearly deleted that last line because it sounds so cliché since MercyMe made it the line of a hit song...) We will see Jesus face to face. In Him we will be made new and in Him all of creation will be redeemed. Even the exclamation point!!!!!! (I typically hate it when people enter repeated exclamation points, but now I see that they are just responding to the sense of inadequacy that they feel when they use that punctuation mark).

[29] 1 Timothy 3:16; Romans 1:4. Note in Romans that the proof that Scripture offers that Jesus is real is the resurrection.

but Jesus is the one who made the original connection in Matthew 12:20, so we'll take it.

In conclusion, we need to deliver what we have received as of first importance. Let us be passionate about evangelism and let our actions reflect a conviction that the delivery of the Gospel message ought to be prioritized.

Let us be careful to get the Gospel right. The Gospel is simple and can be stated simply just as it is deep and can be stated deeply, but there are certain elements that must not be left out and we see them in these two helpful verses in 1 Corinthians 15. As Christians, the Gospel is the foundation of our hope and life. May we proclaim it as such.

Some Related Scripture Passages:

John 1:29

Acts 17:2-3

Romans 3:23-35

1 Corinthians 1:18

2 Corinthians 5:21

Galatians 1:3-4

Galatians 3:13

Colossians 2:15

Hebrews 2:17

1 Peter 2:24

1 John 4:10

Some Quotes:

"Nothing short of the extreme and strong and startling doctrine of the divinity of Christ will give that particular effect that can truly stir the popular sense like a trumpet; the idea of the king himself serving in the ranks of a common soldier. By making that figure merely human we make the story much less human. We take away the point of the story which actually pierces humanity; the point of the story which was quite literally the point of a spear. It does not especially humanise the universe to say that good and wise men can die for their opinions; any more than it would be any sort of uproariously popular news in an army that good soldiers may easily get killed. It is no news that King Leonidas is dead any more than that Queen Anne is dead; and men did not wait for Christianity to be men, in the full sense of being heroes. But if we are describing, for the moment, the atmosphere of what is generous and popular and even picturesque, any knowledge of human nature will tell us that no sufferings of the sons of men, or even of the servants of God, strike the same note as the notion of the master suffering instead of his servants. And this is given by the theological and emphatically not by the scientific deity. No mysterious monarch, hidden in his starry pavilion at the base of the cosmic campaign, is in the least like that celestial chivalry of the Captain who carries his five wounds in the front of the battle." – G. K. Chesterton[30]

"Thankfully, whatever God demands from his children he also supplies to his children in the gospel." - Jared C. Wilson[31]

"When you really believe the gospel, you see that you are first a sinner and only secondarily sinned against." – an anonymous counselor[32]

"How much Thou hast loved us, O good Father, who hast spared not even Thine own Son, but delivered Him up for us wicked men! How Thou hast loved us, for whom He who thought it not robbery to be equal with Thee became obedient even unto death of the cross. He who alone was free among the dead, having power to lay down His life and power to take it up again; for He was to Thee both Victor and Victim, and Victor because Victim: for us He was to Thee both Priest and Sacrifice, and Priest because Sacrifice; turning us from slaves into Thy sons, by being Thy Son and becoming a slave. Rightly is my hope strong in Him, for you will heal all my infirmities through Him who sits at Thy right hand and intercedes for us; otherwise I should despair. For many and great are my infirmities, many and great; but Thy medicine is of more power. We might well have thought Thy Word remote from union with man and so have despaired of

---

[30] G. K. Chesterton, *The Everlasting Man* (San Francisco, CA: Ignatius Press, 1993), 243.

[31] Jared C. Wilson, *Gospel Deeps* (Wheaton, IL: Crossway, 2012), 84.

[32] Quoted in J. D. Greear, *Gospel: Recovering the Power that Made Christianity Revolutionary* (Nashville, TN: B&H Publishing Group, 2011), 114.

ourselves, if It has not been made flesh and dwelt among us." – St. Augustine[33]

Questions for Further Reflection:

1. Is the Gospel neglected in your life and circles of fellowship? Why do we sometimes not treat it as of first importance? Do we just not care? Has the deceiver convinced us that it is not significant? Is there some other reason why? Perhaps multiple reasons to explain it all? Is there anything we can do? What has to change in our disposition to affect a change in our action?[34]

2. "Why didn't God just forgive us? Why did he have to kill someone innocent to satisfy the wrath that is the result of a rule that he made up?" This is a form of a question that I am often asked. It is a good question. How would you answer it?[35]

---

[33] Augustine, *Confessions*, 2nd edition, trans. F. J. Sheed (Indianapolis, IN: Hackett Publishing Company, 2006), 227-228, X.42.69.

[34] This is not to suggest that we work things out on our own. Some may point to this question and say "There's the problem. Luke wants *us* to fix our attitude. That is a works based salvation. We need to just trust the Spirit." It is true that the Spirit works sanctification in us. We are however commanded to live holy lives as we grow more and more in conformity to the image of Christ. As the Spirit sanctifies us he is also redeeming our will. Thus it should not surprise us that, by the gracious work of the Spirit, it would feel like we are choosing to do the right thing as we exercise our being-sanctified will. I am not advocating a works-based salvation or even a works-based sanctification, but I am saying that Scripture gives us a clear responsibility for our actions and the decisions we make.

[35] Here is another good quote from Richard Dawkins for you: "In any case (one can't help wondering), who was God trying to

3. Another good question: "Why should a divine human being, with creation and eternity on his mind, care a fig for petty human malefactions? We humans give ourselves such airs, ever aggrandizing our poky little 'sins' to the level of cosmic significance."[36]

4. To give your brain a break from the previous questions here is a puzzle:

teeemdxlmtopithrdeeecaainon!

---

impress? Presumably himself – judge and jury as well as execution victim. To cap it all, Adam, the supposed perpetrator of the original sin, never existed in the first place: an awkward fact – excusably unknown to Paul but presumably known to an omniscient God (and Jesus, if you believe he was God?) – which fundamentally undermines the premise of the whole tortuously nasty theory, Oh, but of course, the story of Adam and Eve was only ever *symbolic*, wasn't it? *Symbolic?* So, in order to impress himself, Jesus had himself tortured and executed, in vicarious punishment for a *symbolic* sin committed by a *non-existent* individual? As I said, barking mad, as well as viciously unpleasant." (Dawkins, *The God Delusion*, 253)
[36] Dawkins, *The God Delusion*, 238.

2. THE IMPORTANCE OF SCRIPTURE
or THE PURPOSE, PERSPICUITY,[37] SUFFICIENCY, AUTHORITY, AND NECESSITY OF THE INFALLIBLE, INSPIRED, INERRANT SPECIAL[38] REVELATION OF GOD

*"Then Jesus **was led up by the Spirit** into the wilderness*

to be tempted by the devil.

And after fasting forty days and forty nights,

he was hungry.

And the tempter came and said to him,

'If you are the Son of God,

command these stones to become loaves of bread.'

But he answered, 'It is written,

"Man shall not live by bread alone,

but by EVERY word

*that comes from **the mouth of God**."'"*

Matthew 1:1-4

---

[37] I have always thought this was a cruel word to ever use. That being said, I hope you have to look it up.

[38] 'Special' in a technical sense. As opposed to general revelation which is the revelation of God in the world and our experience. We will look a little more at general revelation in the later section on Creation.

You will see in this study an emphasis on Scripture. It is a gift to have God's word lead and guide us by his Spirit. It is the primary way that we know God and what he has done. We want to point others and our own hearts and minds to the Word of God.[39]

Pray & Read: John 17:17; Romans 15:4; Colossians 3:15-17; 2 Timothy 3:14-17

1. According to these verses, what work can Scripture accomplish as God's word?

2. What would you say to someone who did not believe that the Bible is necessary for the Christian life?

3. Are there any ways, whether in prayer or in your thoughts or in your interactions with others or in your daily routine that your actions indicate that you do not fully believe that the Bible is necessary for the Christian life?

4. What does it mean for the word of Christ to "dwell in you richly" (Col. 3:16)?

---

[39] John 1:1-18 (especially verses 1 and 14) I will often use the Word of God in a deliberately ambiguous manner because I believe the Bible points us to the one who is the Word. Similarly, on the basis of John 14 & 16 I believe that we know and encounter Jesus by his Spirit through the Bible. What we know of the Word (Bible) comes from and points to the Word (Jesus) and what we know of the Word (Jesus) comes from and points to the Word (Bible). If that is lacking perspicuity, let's talk.

21

5. How do these passages testify to Christ?

6. What do these passages mean for you as one who is *in Christ?*

7. What are you going to do in response? Who can you get to help you?

FOR FURTHER STUDY

Something to Read

A focus on Christ, *who* is the Word of God,[40] will naturally be accompanied by a focus on Scripture, *which* is the word of God.[41] We primarily know and understand God through his revelation in his Word, that is, through Jesus and through Scripture.[42] Jesus is

---

[40] John 1.

[41] 2 Timothy 3:16

[42] We also know that God is revealed through his creation and through human experience, known as general revelation, but our understanding of general revelation must be guided by the special/particular revelation of God's word. For instance, apart from God's word, suppose you were to examine the complexity of the eye. You could recognize the need for an organizer of such complexity and draw the conclusion that there must be a creator. You might note the variety of eye colors and believe that the creator must also enjoy beauty and variety. You may take it further and theorize that seeing is a means of experiencing the rest of the world and sight itself may be a reflection of the creator's experience as well. However, without the benefit of God's word a lot of other poor conclusions could come from the examination of the eye. One could note that some eyes do not work that well and conclude that the creator is not all that great at doing his work. Or that the eye can experience pain and therefore the creator must be at least a

God revealed to us.[43] Jesus is revealed to us through the Bible. The way that you know that you know something about Jesus is because the Bible tells us that it is so.[44] Scripture is the basis of our understanding of who God is and what he has done.

Similarly, the way that you can know anything is actually the way that you think it is, is if Scripture tells you that it is so.[45] God's word carries the authority of God himself and is therefore authoritative for our very lives. It should be foundational in our faith and the practice of our faith. Speaking from Scripture accurately is the surest way to know that we are speaking truth. Living by the Spirit's power in accordance with a right understanding of the revelation of God in Scripture is the surest way to know that you are living in truth.

"How do we know Scripture is true?"
This is a question that is worth asking. This question has been answered in a variety of ways, but I offer three arguments here. I would say that the first is the most important,[46] and then I am not sure about the order of importance after that because the remaining arguments overlap and work best together.

---

little bit cruel. And on and on. Consider what mosquitoes or the AIDS virus or the prevalence of suffering would say about the creator without the clarifying word of God found in Scripture. This is a similar point that we see in Psalm 8. The psalmist expresses that, apart from God telling him otherwise, he would look that the stars above and conclude that man is not all that significant.

[43] John 1:18; 14:7

[44] The study of how we know what we know is called epistemology. There will be some overlap into epistemology in our discussion here.

[45] This assumes that you have rightly understood Scripture!

[46] It is the foundational argument because it is the surest argument. However, the skeptic will find it the least convincing – but that does not mean it is not the most appropriate starting point!

First, we know it is true because it says it is true. This is the argument from self-attestation. It is definitely a circular argument.[47] But it has to be this way! If God is the final authority, then his words cannot be subjected to any other authority. The basis of the idea is the presupposition that God is the ultimate authority.[48] If any other authority can determine if the word of God is authoritative, then that authority is a higher authority.

This claim is no more circular than any other argument. If you deny that the Bible is authoritative, you are making a judgment on the basis of something else.

---

[47] I say 'definitely,' but I only mean that from a certain point of view. Have you ever taken one of those pictures where you use a sparkler or some other form of light to draw a circle? I think the circularity of this argument is a circle in the same way that the limited, finite snapshot of a camera makes the light into a circle in the moment the picture is taken. However, there is a singular source and starting point to the circle – the light. Likewise, God is the singular source of the authority and he is the one that puts the argument of self-attestation into motion as the source of all truth. So, it is only *kind of* a circle, but it is not hard to see why others would say it looks like a circle if they are just looking at the snapshot of the argument.

[48] In my experience, if a person is not willing to accept *even the possibility* of such a presupposition, no fruitful conversation will follow. So, to gauge the terrain of a person's heart, I may ask "Do you think it is possible that there might be a God capable of revealing himself and that he has done so?" If the person answers that question in the negative, there is a hardness of heart there that is unlikely to be receptive to any argument that needs the listener to be open to the possibility of the existence of God. That being said, that person is not a lost cause. Romans 1:18 let's us know that all people know the truth of God's existence, but suppress the truth. There's something else going on with this person that is not an intellectual objection but an objection of the heart. Again, Scripture tells us as much, "The fool says *in his heart*, 'There is no God'" (Psalm 14:1, emphasis mine). Be a friend and love that person. Let the love of Christ in you shine as you serve as a minister of reconciliation to them (2 Corinthians 5:16-21). Perhaps the love of Christ in you will be used to warm their hardness of heart.

Perhaps you do not like what it says, or the implications it carries for how you would live your life, or you reject it because it contains miracles and strange events that 'just don't happen.'[49] Whatever that 'something else' is, you cannot prove that it ought to be the final authority; you can only *presuppose* that it should be so.[50]

Second, is the Bible's correspondence to reality. This is the argument that easily fits into how we naturally evaluate truth claims. It is the simple test that we intuitively apply to everything. Does this seem true? Does this align with our experience? We have likely all had times when we have misunderstood our experience, but by and large our experience corresponds to reality. If I think it is raining outside because the conditions of my previous experience (it is dark and cloudy and water is coming out of the sky when it rains) correspond to my current experience of seeing it be dark and cloudy and water-falling-from-the-sky, then I could reasonably conclude that it is raining. I may be wrong. It may not be a window I am actually looking at but a digital screen. Or perhaps I am in a dream and looking out a window. Or perhaps René Descartes was correct in his *Meditations on First*

---

[49] It is noteworthy that miracles and events are recorded in the Bible for exactly the reason that such things 'just don't happen.' That is why it having happened is so remarkable. It is not that ancient people were more susceptible to believing extraordinary things. It is exactly because they were not that they recorded the remarkable miracles found in Scripture. If virgin births are happening all the time it is hardly newsworthy.

[50] Thus, we can appeal to a person to lay aside existing presuppositions in order to consider the presupposition that Scripture *might be true* in order to rightly consider its claims.

Philosophy and there is a malicious demon[51] toying with my perception.[52]

Scripture does indeed explain our existence. The truths it offers conform to the reality of the world we see and experience. In my experience, no other book can better help me understand my experience of life. Neither the Qur'an, the meditations of Marcus Aurelius, Taoism, the tenets of faith of the Sunni, Shia, Sufi, and Sikh, the claims of *The Book of Mormon* and *The Pearl of Great Price*, the wisdom of Buddha and Confucius, nor the tales of the Bhagavad-Gita nor the morals of the humanist or non-Messianic Jew have satisfied me. But I can read the first three chapters of Genesis and see the story of creation, fall, and the promise of redemption and hear something that explains the world I experience. Consider all that we gather from Genesis 1-3 as the Bible:

- Explains the good we see in the world – God made the world good.

- Explains the bad we see and feel and do – Sin entered the world through man's rebellion.

- Explains our desire for companionship – we were not meant to be alone, God made us in his

---

[51] Is there any other kind of demon?

[52] Consider the implication that even in these misconceptions, we see a distorted reality. Arguably, the existence of a distorted reality points to a true reality – whether I am aware of the true reality or not. While that is an interesting philosophical situation to consider, it is ultimately unhelpful because we are only concerned with the truth that we can know. A true reality that cannot be known cannot, hang with me here, be known. So there is little reason to try to know it. If you get this concept, then you get why we are dependent on God revealing himself to us and you have just seen yet another reason why Scripture is so important. God is a true reality that can be known because he has made it possible for himself to be known.

image to reflect community (the one, triune God is perfect community within himself).

- Explains our sense of estrangement – we were meant to have good relationships with God and people but that has been broken.

- Explains our sense of discontentment – the life that we live is not the ideal for which we were made by God.

- Explains why we like redemption in our stories and take notice when no redemption is found or offered – there is a longing for redemption within us.[53]

- Explains the universal awareness of the divine – we were made to live in a relationship with God, the world's religions point to this awareness and seek to regain that relationship.

- Gives a basis for valuing life – all people were created by God in his image.

- Eliminates a basis for racism, but explains why it still exists – we were *all* made in his image, but have fallen and now live in strife and enmity with one another.

- Explains why work can be both satisfying and hard and why childbirth is both painful and

---

[53] Such a longing betrays the fact that we know things are not the way they are supposed to be. One of the reasons I love the short stories of Flannery O'Conner is because she uses the grotesque to show us into awareness of our desire for things to be made right. Interestingly, Cormac McCarthy ends up doing a similar thing in his stories (if you have not read him, perhaps you have seen the movie adaptation of *No Country for Old Men),* but he does not do so from a position of Christian faith.

joyous – we were made for work and to be fruitful and multiply but we live in a fallen world where sin, death, and the curse are realities.

- Shows us God's grace and his promise of redemption – a seed of the woman will come to face the serpent.

If Scripture explains the world so well, when taken to be true, that is a meaningful indicator that it is true.

Third, is the idea of "faith seeking understanding."[54] There is a lot of overlap here with the second case for the truthfulness of Scripture, but it is worth examining on its own. As St. Augustine explains, "understanding is the reward of faith. Therefore do not seek to understand in order to believe, but believe that though mayest understand."[55] It is the idea that if you take Scripture to be true, you end up seeing that it is true.[56] Faith is rewarded with understanding. This is not necessarily a compelling argument for a non-believer, but for a believer in doubt, it is helpful.[57] We must

---

[54] St. Anselm coined the phase 'faith seeking understanding' (Latin: *fides quaerens intellectum*) in his *Proslogion*. St. Augustine, a couple centuries before Anselm, had a similar idea – believe that you may understand – that he discusses in his homily on John in *Tractate* 29.6.
[55] Augustine, "Tractate XXIX" in *Nicene and Post-Nicene Fathers: Augustin – Gospel of John, First Epistle of John, Soliloquies*, vol 7, trans. John Gibb and James Innes, ed. Philip Schaff (Peabody, MA: Hendrickson Publishers, 2012), 184.
[56] I have several Mormons make the same argument for their faith. It may be an argument that belongs to other religions. For that reason, it clearly is not the ultimate proof, but it is valuable combined with the other arguments.
[57] J. D. Greear once told me that Charles Spurgeon said "doubt is a foot poised." You can either take a step forward or a step backward. Doubt is not bad in and of itself, but is an opportunity. I'm not sure where the quote comes from. I see something similar in Spurgeon's

insist that Scripture be taken on its own terms and in its own categories, but if you do that, take Scripture at face-value and see where that takes you.

It is not surprising that sinful man will be reluctant to accept proofs that point to the truthfulness of God's word. Consider the crowd in John 12:23-29 that heard the distinct and clear voice of God validating that Jesus is who he says is his and yet disregarded the sound of God's voice as merely thunder. Or look at the guards at the tomb who experienced the evidence of the resurrection of Jesus first-hand, but chose to spread a lie.[58] If seeing is not always believing, we should not be surprised when people reject the truth claims of Scripture.[59]

"Does Scripture have errors in it?"
In 2003, I was in the Athenian marketplace when a shop owner struck up a conversation with me. He wanted to know why I was in Greece and he was curious about what I was learning during my study tour of the country. Constantinatius offered me my choice of one of his fine carpets if I could correctly answer one question. I excitedly accepted the challenge and reached for the Bible in my back pocket[60] when he asked, "who was the father of Joseph the father of Jesus?" I turned to Matthew, read Matthew 1:16 to

---

volume 3 of *Lectures to my Students*, but cannot find the exact quote. Just the same, it's a fantastic point!
[58] Matthew 28:11-15.
[59] Proofs for the validity of Scripture are still important. They demonstrate the rationality of belief and the irrationality of disbelief. But we cannot expect proofs to, without fail, change lives. Proofs for the supernatural will always point to the supernatural. A worldview that rejects the supernatural will reject supernatural proofs. But if only natural proofs are accepted you can only expect it to point to the natural.
[60] I still have that small Bible, but it's now easier to just carry a Bible in my front pocket on my phone.

myself, and answered "Jacob" as I began to turn my eye towards his selection of handcrafted Turkish-rugs. "Wrong! Look at Luke 3:23."[61] I turned the pages in my small Bible and read to myself "Jesus...being the son (as was supposed) of Joseph, the son of Heli." Seeing the look of surprise in my face, Constantinatius launched into a speech about the failures and inaccuracies of the Bible and its overall inferiority to Greek thought and philosophy. His harangue culminated with him saying that he would rather follow the one that took the cup of hemlock and drank it to his death[62] than follow the one who – and he got down on his knees and looked towards the heavens in mockery – cries "Father, take this cup from me."[63] I was so ashamed of my failure and walked away grieving that I had failed to defend my Lord, but I was also confused.

Having had that experience, and grown from it, I still affirm that the Bible is the infallible, inspired, inerrant word of God. The Bible does not fail us as it comes from God and he is the one who never fails.[64] It is inerrant in that it is truth without the mixture of error. This inerrancy is true of translations and copies of Scripture insofar as they faithfully communicate the

---

[61] "It's a trap!" – Admiral Ackbar

[62] An allusion to Socrates who was sentenced to drink a poisonous cup of hemlock for corrupting the youth with his philosophy. You can find the account in Plato's *Apology* – "Now the hour to part has come. I go to die, you go to live. Which of us goes to the better lot is known to no one, except the god." Plato, *Plato: Complete Works*, trans. G. M. A. Grube, ed. John M. Cooper (Indianapolis, IN: Hackett Publishing Company, 1997), 35.

[63] An allusion to Christ in the garden of Gethsemane in Matthew 26:39.

[64] This is the implication of inspiration and the meaning of infallibility. 'Infallibility' became a contested term that ended up having a confusing variety of definitions. So 'inerrant' has become the word of choice for (many/most) orthodox Christians. However, that term has started to have it's own challenges to it as well.

original text.[65] This does not mean that we take everything literally in the Bible without regard for literary forms and the historical literary standards of its day(s).

The doctrine of inerrancy is not a recent doctrine, nor is it a recently challenged doctrine. You find an assumption of the truth of Scripture throughout the Patristic period. It is the same in the medieval period. The Reformation revolt against Rome was an issue of fidelity to Scripture that is based on the understanding that Scripture speaks truthfully. Confessions of faith from the early church on through the Reformation and up to today speak to the belief of the truthfulness of Scripture. The challenges to inerrancy arguably go back to the serpent uttering, "Has God really said?"[66] Those that challenge the inerrancy of Scripture have an authority issue. What authority is there to judge Scripture if it is not judged by the authority of God?[67]

You may hear Christians explain that Scripture is inspired, and is therefore inerrant, and therefore it is authoritative. I think it is better to start with authority. If one can presuppose that there might be a God and that he might have revealed himself, then the argument from authority is a solid argument. God is the source of all things, so all truth comes from him. The authority of God in Christ leads to the doctrine of

---

[65] 'God is love' vs. "God loves Lucas' – the reason that the first is received as inspired, inerrant, and authoritative is because it was written by the apostle John under the Holy Spirit (1 John 4:8). The second is a true conclusion from God's word, but it is not God's word.
[66] Genesis 3:1.
[67] How about the challenge of experience? How about the law of non-contradiction that states A cannot both be B and not be B? To state it another way, the father of Joseph the (supposed) father of Jesus cannot be Heli and not-Heli (Jacob). If you want to read more: Book Gamma of Aristotle's *Metaphysics*.

inspiration, which leads to inerrancy. Thus we say that we know Scripture is inerrant because it comes from God not that we know it is from God because it is inerrant.

Demonstrating a lack of error in Scripture is a significant way of demonstrating authority, but ultimately a person has to recognize the authority of (or behind or in) Scripture before they will accept the inerrancy of Scripture. Anything can be explained away. I can believe that Matthew and Luke each account a true genealogy of Christ. One traces the line through Mary and the other through Joseph and that speaking of Mary in a genealogy as her husband 'Joseph' was a culturally acceptable norm. But that explanation is not going to work for someone who has a problem with the authority of the Bible, nor will any other explanation that does not deny the inerrancy of Scripture.[68]

"But other scriptures make the claim to being God's revelation? How do we know we have the right one(s)?" As far as the Bible as a whole, this goes back to self-attestation, correspondence to experience, and faith seeking understanding. In regards to the canon[69] and the self-attestation argument specifically, consider John 14-16 (especially 14:18, 25-22; 16:13-15) and the claim of Jesus that the Spirit would guide the communities of

---

[68] People do not like authority and that it is why it is so hard to talk about inerrancy with those who have not been born again. Ever since Eden, people have been trying to live as gods (Genesis 3:5). Apart from Jesus, we are the prodigal son, wanting the benefits of being a son without living under the father's love and authority. The Spirit of God must act if a person is to believe and submit to the authority of God. Through the Spirit we see that subjection to the authority of God is freedom to live as we were meant to live. It is a blessing and not a curse. The curse is the lonely, oppressive individualization of the one who rejects the authority of God.

[69] The accepted books/contents of the Bible that make up Scripture.

faith to the truth. The faithful, Christ-honoring communities will be nourished by the Spirit that relays God's word. The true Scriptures of faith are going to be the Scriptures that Jesus said they would be – the writings delivered by the Spirit that are left with the faithful disciples of God.

Many will make other arguments for the canonization of Scripture, most of which will point to apostolic authority as the guide.[70] Personally, I find those arguments a little dissatisfying if separated from the argument that the authority is evidenced by Spirit-filled, Christ-honoring communities springing up from the text. Bart Ehrman has made a lot of money and has had a successful career by poking at the argument for the canon from apostolic authority. He writes:

Where did we get our New Testament Gospels in the first place, and how do we know that *they*, rather than the dozens of Gospels that did *not* become part of the New Testament, reveal the truth about what Jesus taught? What if the canon had ended up containing the Gospels of Peter, Thomas, and Mary rather than Matthew, Mark, and Luke?[71]

Ehrman has a point that is difficult to counter when competing claims to apostolic authority are made by a number of the books outside of the canon.[72] However,

---

[70] Written by an apostle or someone close to an apostle.
[71] Bart D. Ehrman, *Lost Christianities: The Battles for Scripture and the Faiths We Never Knew* (NY: Oxford University Press, 2003), 93. This book, *Jesus, Interrupted: Revealing the Hidden Contradictions in the Bible (and Why We Don't Know About Them)*, and *Lost Scriptures: Books that Did Not Make It into the New Testament* are the only books by Ehrman I have read (the last is really just a collection of non-canonical texts). Best I can tell, nearly all of his books make the same argument, just in slightly different ways.
[72] Not that those are actually written by the apostles as they claim to be.

the primary force of that argument melts away if your criterion for the canon is the self-attesting John 14-16.[73]

A few other challenges to the importance and inerrancy of Scripture, real quick!
Some argue that the Bible is only inerrant in matters of faith and practice. They argue that it tells the truth when it comes to matters of how to be saved or grow in godliness, but it is not necessarily true in matters related to science, history, or philosophy. The problem with this view is that Scripture loses all authority by association. Faith is contingent upon historical events, thus the Bible has to be historically accurate.

Some argue that the doctrine of inerrancy is just a modern idea. While the terminology may be recent, the meaning is not. But even if it were a modern idea, one still needs to demonstrate why the doctrine of inerrancy is not key to our understanding of revelation.

Some point out that we no longer have the originals as problematic.[74] This argument is subtly woven into arguments employed by Ehrman. This really is not an issue if you presuppose that there is a God capable of revealing himself and preserving that revelation. If you accept that possibility, then the scenario we have (of not having the originals two thousand years later) is neither surprising nor problematic.

---

[73] Ehrman could, and does, still counter that the canon is the result of the victors writing history, but this goes back to presuppositions. However, you have to make an addition to the question we have asked: "Do you believe that there could be a God capable of revealing himself, that he has, and that he is capable of preserving his revelation?" If there answer to this is "no" you can never have an argument in which you will convince Dr. Ehrman, for the reasons already given above.
[74] You may sometimes hear the original manuscripts referred to as the 'autographs.'

In conclusion, God's word is important. He has given it to us to reveal himself and truth is attached to every aspect of God's word. You can affirm God's word is true and also recognize that it may not conform to modern standards of statistical precision,[75] nor historiographical precision in genealogies,[76] nor cosmological terminology,[77] nor today's standards for verbal exactitude in its quotations.[78] We can affirm the truth of Scripture while recognizing that it employs metaphorical and literary means of conveying truth – imagery, symbols, etc. So let us not ignore Scripture. The Bible should impact the way we pray and worship. It should shape our thoughts and actions. We cannot have too much Scripture in our lives and it is likely that we too often have too little.

Some Related Scripture Passages:

Numbers 12

Deuteronomy 18:15-22

2 Samuel 7:28

Psalm 19

John 14; 16; 17:17

Hebrews 1:1-2

---

[75] Numbers may be summarized and rounded.

[76] The pointing the genealogies is rarely exact recordkeeping, but instead something theological.

[77] Even modern man still utilizes the phenomenological expression that the 'sun sets" even though we know that the sun is not moving at all.

[78] Start looking up the original verses of the Old Testament quoted in the New Testament and you will see what I mean. There is a reason for the differences, but this section is already long enough!

1 John 1:1-4

Some Quotes:

"When I was a boy I thought I had found a thousand contradictions in the Bible. In the Old Bible of my young manhood I marked them all. Well, I had then nearly a thousand more contradictions than I have now. I do not see them now; they are not there. There are perhaps a half dozen in the Bible that I cannot explain satisfactorily to myself. I don't say that my explanation of all the others would satisfy everybody. There are some that I cannot explain satisfactorily to myself; but since I have seen nine hundred and ninety-four out of those thousand coalesce and harmonize like two streams mingling, I am disposed to think that if I had more sense I could harmonize those other six; and even if I ever fail to harmonize them, God knows better than I know, and that when I know perfectly just as I now know only in part, and only a very small part, I will be able to understand that; and so when I come to things of that kind and cannot master them, I put them in parenthesis and say, 'I will come back; God cannot leave you penned forever; He will send somebody that can take away the difficulty and make it clear to me.' I assume that it can be done."– B. H. Carroll[79]

"In the New Testament only one word per 1,000 is in any way doubtful, and no point of doctrine is lost when verses not 'in better manuscripts' are omitted. (As examples, see Matt. 6:13b, 17:21, 18:11; Mark 9:44, 16:9-20; Luke 23:17; John 5:4; and Acts 8:37.) Such has been God's 'singular care and providence' in

---

[79] B. H. Carroll, *Inspiration of the Bible.* (Nashville: Thomas Nelson, 1980), 121.

preserving his written Word for us (Westminster Confession I.viii)." – J. I. Packer[80]

Questions for Further Reflection:

1. Are some sections of Scripture more important than others? If so, in what sense? How do you know which sections are more important? If not, how is that reflected in your study and approach to the Bible?

2. Is our knowledge of God limited to Scripture? If so, is that limiting him and putting him in a box that reduces our experience of the revelation he has offered to a single book? If not, how can you gauge what is true knowledge of God?

3. Do you believe that there are any errors in the Bible? If yes, then how do you know what those errors are? If no, how can you be sure?

4. Who was the father of Joseph the father of Jesus? (Matthew 1:16; Luke 3:23) Who worked in David's heart to order a census? (2 Samuel 24:1; 1 Chronicles 21:1) How did Judas die? (Matthew 27:5; Acts 1:18) Why hasn't Jesus come back yet? (Matt 24:34; Mark 13:30; Luke 21:32) What are we to make of these things?

5. I have heard at least one middle school camper argue that Scripture was not all true. He believed that it had been corrupted over the years as it was handed

---

[80] J. I. Packer. "Good Question: Text Criticism and Inerrancy" in *Christianity Today*. October 7, 2002.

down.[81] He used the telephone game to illustrate his point that if you get a bunch a people to pass along a piece of information one person at a time it becomes corrupted. How would you respond to this argument?

6. How would you respond to someone who told you that it is absurd to believe that Scripture is literally true since it tells of resurrections, floating ax-heads, and world-wide floods? Do you answer with evidence to support those things? Do you respond with arguments favoring the presence of a supernatural deity? Do you say it just takes faith? Do you respond by sharing the Gospel? What would be your response?

7. Is the Bible the Word of God or is it merely a witness to the Word of God?

8. Is the authority of God in the Bible challenged by science?

---

[81] Islam makes the same claim. They believe that the Scriptures we have were once the true revelation of Allah, but they have been corrupted over time. As the story goes, Allah sent a corrected and updated revelation of himself, the Qu'ran, through the prophet Muhammad.

3. THE STORY OF SCRIPTURE (& HISTORY & YOUR LIFE) IS UNDERSTOOD IN RELATION TO JESUS THE CHRIST

"Then he said to them,

'These are my words that I spoke to you while I was still

with you, that everything written about me

in the Law of Moses and the Prophets and the Psalms

must be fulfilled.'

*Then he **opened their minds** to understand Scripture."*

Luke 24:44-45

There is a benefit to understanding the big picture when trying to rightly interpret and apply any given story. It adds depth to meaning. In the same way that I understand old episodes of Lost[82] better after having seen the most recent episodes, so also I can pick up on things in Scripture when I go back through it as I grow in my understanding of the overall plot.[83]

I have also found that knowing God's overall plan helps me trust Him with what He is doing with my

---

[82] Dated reference – I know! But it was the most confusing show I ever watched and in the end (unlike Scripture) it was a total waste of my time! Seriously.

[83] Warning: another super dated reference… If you know Bruce Willis's character is dead, you watch the movie *The Sixth Sense* differently. If you do not get this reference or the last, go watch a snapchat story or a youtube or something.

life. To be certain, I fail to trust Him often, but there are times when I am reminded that there is something bigger going on here than just what I want.

Pray & Read: John 1:43-51; Luke 24:13-48; 2 Corinthians 1:19-22; 1 Peter 1:10-12

1. What stands out to you in these passages?

2. Jesus and the NT writers see Jesus (and his work) as the fulfillment of things written about Jesus in the Law, Prophets, and Psalms. In Luke 24:45 Jesus opens the minds of the disciples to understand the Scriptures. Do these texts suggest that seeing the role of Jesus in fulfilling OT texts is the key to understanding the Scriptures? If so, summarize the point from all four of the passages listed. If not,[84] carefully summarize what is necessary to understand the Scriptures.

3. What does the Spirit mean, when he tells us through Paul in 2 Corinthians 1:20, that *all* the promises of God find their Yes *in* the Son of God, Jesus Christ? Try to think through this concretely. Since it says 'all' perhaps list some promises of God and write out how those promises find their Yes *in* Jesus.

4. According to 1 Peter 1:10-12, what was uncertain to the prophets? What was certain to them? How is your understanding of their prophecies now more complete?

---

[84] While I am arguing for "If so" I can see the possibility of a few carefully nuanced "If not" explanations.

5. How do these passages testify to Christ?

6. What do these passages mean for you as one who is *in Christ?*

7. What are you going to do in response? Who can you get to help you?

FOR FURTHER STUDY

Something to Read

In the summer of 2008[85] for Guys Staff Bible Study[86] at CWR we covered the storyline of Scripture. We looked at it during Staff Training. I wanted to cover it early on because I think it is foundational to shaping how one understands Scripture and seeks to think through things biblically. I told the guys that we were going to cover the whole Bible and I remember that there was an apprehensive air as we began the study. It was at night and we didn't start until late in the evening. We prayed and I told them to open their Bibles. Anywhere was fine, because we would be covering it all. There were some nervous laughs, as it had already been quite a long day and everyone was understandably looking forward to some sleep, but then we jumped in.[87] At the end of the summer a couple of guys approached me about that night. They told me that there was a change in their whole approach to Bible study and their

---

[85] Back in the good old days!
[86] GSBS, except for when 'GSBS' is 'Girls Staff Bible Study'
[87] Really, they were so concerned about how long we were going to be and I can't blame them! Half of them didn't know me yet. Which, I don't know if that would have made them more or less afraid of what was to come.

outlook on life that began during that 40-minute lesson. I am not trying to recreate the magic here or promise that I am getting ready to change your life.[88] What I am trying to do is share with you truth from Scripture that changed me, but took me way too long to realize.

So a couple of things:

The NT says that the OT points to Christ.[89]
The Gospels say that they are about Christ.[90]
The Acts speak about the expansion of his kingdom as the church grows.
The epistles are about the life of those in the kingdom.[91]
And, finally, Revelation is "the revelation of Jesus Christ."[92]

So, the Bible is about Jesus.[93] This means that the storyline of Scripture is about Jesus Christ in some way or another. If you try to understand Scripture apart from Christ, then you will misunderstand it. It is like trying to watch a 3-D movie without the 3-D glasses – things will be blurry, hard to understand, and might give you a headache.

---

[88] Though the prideful part of me (that is being put to death by the Spirit), does want to do that.
[89] Luke 24:44-45; John 1:43-51; 1 Pet. 1:10-12
[90] Matthew, Mark, Luke, John.
[91] You can read the opening few verses of almost any of the epistles and you will get the idea.
[92] Revelation 1:1.
[93] Some more verses on the central focus of Scripture on Christ: John 5:39 is a zinger; John 5:46; Acts 10:43 states that *all* the prophets bear witness to Jesus; to a lesser degree you have affirmations of the centrality of Christ in Ephesians 1:9-10; Hebrews 1:1-3ff; Matthew 2:4-6; Luke 2:25-26.

There are benefits to knowing the whole picture. One of those benefits is that knowing the whole gives us context when we study any of the part. Any text of Scripture we read we want to understand it in context and there are at least three contexts: textual, epochal, and canonical.[94] The textual context is the immediate context around the verses or passage that you are studying. We should not pull a meaning from a verse or a passage that is out of place or inconsistent with the meaning of that verse in relation to the verses around it.[95] The epochal context is the context of that passage

---

[94] This approach was first introduced to me by Stephen J. Wellum when I was a student of his in 2007. The terminology of the textual, epochal, and canonical 'horizons' was introduced and developed by Richard Lints in *The Fabric of Theology: A Prolegomenon of Evangelical Theology.*
[95] Two popular examples: Philippians 4:13 ("I can do all things through Christ who strengthens me") is in the context of rejoicing in need and being content in every type of circumstance whether good or poor. In all kinds of circumstances Paul says he can rejoice and be content through Jesus who gives him strength. That's not quite the same message as "I can do another pushup because I can do all things through Christ who gives me strength." But take heart if you have been misapplying this verse out of context! With a small tweak you can say "by the power of Christ in whom I live and move and have my being (Acts 17:28) and through whom I am created and in whom I am held together (Col. 1:16-17) I have life and I intend to do this next pushup!" | Jeremiah 29:11 ("For I know the plans I have for you, declares the LORD, plans for wholeness and not for evil, to give you a future and a hope.") A lot of people have this as a life verse. That's great and I totally encourage it! But don't let it be your life verse apart from its context. The textual context is that Jeremiah is writing to exiles who are probably wondering if God has abandoned them and are wondering if God will ever fulfill his promises as they sit in the foreign land of an oppressor. The LORD, through Jeremiah, is affirming that he has not forgotten his promises and he will one day restore the people to the land and fulfill his promises. These promises include the coming of an obedient son of God who will redeem and restore a people from Israel and the nations (more on this to come). If you are in Jesus, you are *in* the one who is the fulfillment of the promise of Jeremiah 29:11 and thus Jeremiah 29:11 appropriately applies to you. This is a rare instance where keeping Jeremiah 29:11 in its

in relation to when it occurred in redemptive history and what it could mean for the people of God *up to that point* in history.[96] We have an example of this in Romans 4 as Paul argues certain conclusions regarding justification by faith on the basis that Genesis 15:6 occurs before Genesis 17.[97] The canonical context focuses on the meaning of a passage in light of the whole witness of Scripture. This is where it is especially helpful to know the big picture of Scripture and to understand that it is related to Jesus.[98]

---

textual, epochal, and canonical context includes a meaning that aligns with its common out-of-context application. But taking a verse out of context does not always work out so well.

[96] So you will have to pay attention to where the text falls in redemptive history. Hopefully our study of Creation, Fall, Redemption, New Creation will help you place passages in their appropriate epoch/era. Precision is not always required to make meaningful conclusions, but accuracy is. The more you spend time reading Scripture the more familiar you will become with the different epochs and the varied divisions of epochs that exist in Scripture. For instance, you have the division of the Old and New Testaments into two epochs. You could read Matthew 1 and see epochs of Creation to Abraham, Abraham to David, Solomon to Exile, Exile to Christ. (Graeme Goldsworthy follows and advocates this structure in his *According to Plan*). You might notice in the OT that you have the Patriarchs (Abraham, Isaac, Jacob), then Moses , then the conquest, the judges, the kings, exile, and life after exile. You could read Romans and see an epoch of Adam and an epoch of Christ. Or pick up on pre-Law and post-Law divisions of epochs. 1 Peter gives us epochs of pre-Flood, post-Flood, and New Creation. There are many more, but the main idea is to know where you are in the unfolding story.

[97] Two other easy examples: Galatians 3 draws conclusions on the basis that Genesis 15:6 occurs before the giving of the Law. Hebrews 3-4 explores how the word of Moses carried various degrees of similar implications in Moses' day, Joshua's day, the-psalmist-of-Psalm-22's day, and the day of the author of Hebrews.

[98] The book of Hebrews is one of the clearest examples of this in practice (though the canon of Scripture for the writer of Hebrews was smaller than our canon...because, and don't let this confuse you, he was in a different epoch than us).

Another benefit to knowing the big picture is that it adds depth of meaning to any passage of Scripture. When you read a passage of Scripture in light of its context you are reading it in a manner that the New Testament authors themselves read and interpreted Scripture. It opens up the text, not by reading additional things into it, but by seeing how it connects to all other texts. It's a richness and depth that is evident with every Spirit-guided reading of the Bible.

Finally, another benefit of knowing the whole picture is that it not only gives you a better understanding of God's plan, but it also gives you a better understanding of God's plan for your life.[99] We find our story within his story.[100]

To take it a step further...
The story of all of history, not just Scripture, is about Christ. He is the center of all things. He is the reason that everything exists and He is the point of all history. All things find their meaning in Christ. I do not believe that there is anything in the world that can be rightly understood apart from how it is related to Christ. There is not anything, whether in Scripture or in the world, that does not either testify to Christ or testify to the need for Christ.[101] Even our own individual end is to be conformed to the image of Christ.[102]

It is all about Him. Apparently, the plan has always been "to unite all things in Him."[103] Everything is made

---

[99] This is why each week will include a question of "What does this passage mean for you as one who is in Christ?"
[100] Galatians 2:20; Colossians 1:16-17; 1 Peter 1:10-12;
[101] Feel free to test me on this next time you see me! Point to something or mention a situation or passage of Scripture or whatever and we can talk about how it points us to Jesus.
[102] Romans 8:29; 1 John 3:2.
[103] Ephesians 1:10.

through Him and made for Him.[104] And it is in Him that "we live and move and have out being."[105] I am made a co-heir with Christ and I reason to be excited as I am adopted as a son and made co-heir with the heir of all things.[106]

Dr. Russell Moore makes this statement:

> Every text of Scripture – Old or New
> Testaments – is thus about Jesus, precisely
> because, at the end of the day, everything in
> reality is about Jesus. Why is there something
> instead of nothing? Why are human beings
> religious? Why do people want food and water
> and sex and community? Why are there
> galaxies and quasars and blue whales and local
> churches? God is creating all that is for His heir,
> for the glory of Jesus Christ. When you see
> through Jesus, you see the interpretive grid
> through which all of reality makes sense.[107]

I think that's a good statement. When we abstract Scripture from story of Christ we run the risk of developing a Christ-less Christianity We cannot abstract morals and truths apart from Christ and honor God. When the rich young ruler asked how he could have eternal life, he wanted to keep the law apart from obedience to Jesus.[108] When Jesus spoke to Martha about resurrection she referred to a general resurrection of the dead. He wanted her to see that *he*

---

[104] Colossians 1:16-17.
[105] Acts 17:28.
[106] Romans 8:17.
[107] Russel D. Moore, "Beyond a Veggie Tales Gospel: Why We Must Preach Christ From Every Text" accessed at
https://www.russellmoore.com/2008/05/19/beyond-a-veggie-tales-gospel-why-we-must-preach-christ-from-every-text/ on March 16, 2019.
[108] Luke 18:18-30.

is the resurrection and the life.[109] The devil in the wilderness offered Christ a kingdom apart from the cross and the tomb; he tried to tempt Jesus away from the God-ordained and planned story of Christ.[110] So-called 'health and wealth' gospels seek to offer blessings of God apart from the fulfillment of those promises in Christ and according to his plan.

Each week you will see a question along the lines of "How does this passage testify to Christ?" This question will get easier to answer the more time you spend in Scripture and the more often you answer it. It is always a worthwhile question to ask of any passage. There will be a lot of different types of answers that you may see as you study, but here are some considerations to get you started:[111]

- A passage may directly say something about Jesus. This is the easiest instance in which to identify how a passage testifies to Christ.

- A passage may be communicating a promise of God or a fulfillment of a promise of God. If all the promises of God find their yes in Jesus, then there must be a connection.[112]

---

[109] John 11:23-25.
[110] Matthew 4:8-11.
[111] For more options and information, consider Graeme Goldsworthy's excellent *Gospel-Centered Hermeneutics: Foundations and Principles of Evangelical Interpretation*. If you are looking for something lighter, *Christ from Beginning to End: How the Full Story of Scripture Reveals the Full Glory of Christ* by Trent Hunter & Stephen Wellum is another excellent resource that is less technical.
[112] An obscure example to help you see this at work: The lists of names in Numbers (and throughout the OT) that relay how many people belong to each tribe of Israel. It's textual context is that we have a record of how many people belonged to each tribe around

- A passage may reveal our need for Jesus. Jesus may not be presented as the answer in that passage's immediate textual or epochal context, but the canonical context offers Jesus as the answer to our needs.

- A passage may demonstrate a way in which God likes to work. When this happens, consider if Christ would later demonstrate a similar (but often greater) working of God.

Some Related Scripture Passages:

Luke 24

John 1:43-51

Acts 2, 7, 13, 17:26-31[113]

Ephesians 1:3-10

Colossians 1:15-19

Hebrews 1:1-4

1 Peter 1:10-12

Revelation 22:13 with Isaiah 44:4, 6; 48:12

---

the time of the wilderness following the Exodus from Egypt. These lists testify to Christ as a record of God's fulfillment of promises to Abraham in Genesis 12, 15, and 17 to make him a great nation. These lists in Numbers reveal a partial fulfillment of these promises and give us reason to look forward to the ultimate fulfillment of the promise to Abraham in Jesus as the promised seed through whom all the families of the earth will one day be blessed.

[113] Note the way the various speakers in these texts see the culmination of God's redemptive plan as occurring in Jesus.

Some Quotes:

"The kingdom Jesus announced also shows us that we are working within the framework of spiritual warfare, and we ought then to expect opposition and suffering. The structure of the universe, the covenants of Israel, the kings, prophets, and institutions of God's people all picture ahead of time, in varying ways, the life of Christ Jesus. The life of the church pictures the same things, after the fact. Jesus reprises the story of Israel, from anointing to temptation to exile. And he tells us that we will walk in the same way – from the Bethlehem of our new birth to the Jerusalem of our new reign. But in between we will follow him to the Place of the Skull. We will carry our crosses. In order to be glorified with him later, we must suffer with him first (Rom. 8:17). Turning the other cheek leaves you with two broken jaws, but Jesus is still King, and still right." – Russell D. Moore[114]

"The point has to be emphasized that both Old Testament and New Testament bear truthful witness to Jesus Christ in different ways, and that both of their witnesses are measured in the light of the reality of Christ himself." – Brevard S. Childs[115]

Questions for Further Reflection:

---

[114] Russell D. Moore, *Onward: Engaging the Culture Without Losing the Gospel* (Nashville, TN: B&H Publishing Group, 2015), 64.
[115] Brevard S. Childs, *Biblical Theology of the Old and New Testaments: Theological Reflection on the Christian Bible* (Minneapolis, MN: Fortress Press, 2011), 477.

1. People have suggested that the story of
    Scripture is to be seen in light of various centers.
    Jonathan Edwards[116] and John Piper[117] suggest
    that everything in Scripture should be seen
    with a view towards God's glory. Friedrich
    Schleiermacher and Rob Bell[118] see the
    "experience of God" as the lens through which
    all else should be understood. For Martin
    Luther it was justification by faith. Some say
    Scripture should be interpreted primarily in
    light of God's preference for the poor.[119] Others
    say that the center should be a personal
    relationship with God, or how to get wealthy,
    or how to be a better person, or how to get to
    heaven. I have suggested that Christ is to be
    viewed as the center by which, not only
    Scripture, but all of life is to be understood. Do
    you agree? If not, what do you see as the
    central point of Scripture? Why?

---

[116] Edwards applies this to his life as well. Check out his
"Resolutions" and see how many times he mentions the glory of
God.

[117] This theme is throughout Piper's teachings and writings, but his
Don't Waste Your Life is an excellent introduction to the idea. I do
not disagree with Piper, but he often speaks of the glory of God in a
general way and I wish he would more carefully define what he
means. John 12:36-43 identifies the glory of God as Jesus, and while
John Piper likely knows that, it is not often conveyed in his
teaching.

[118] Decades ago people used to talk a lot more about Schleiermacher
than they do now. Similarly, a decade ago a lot of people where
talking about Rob Bell, but you do not hear about him as much
anymore. I bring them up because it is likely that in your lifetime
someone will bring up a similar idea once again and you might as
well be prepared for it.

[119] See Gustavo Gutiérrez's *The Power of the Poor in History* and José
Miguez's *The Theology of Liberation* if this concept is interesting to
you. I disagree with their focus, but believe they reignite an
awareness that Scripture is not silent regarding the poor and the
oppressed.

2. Allegorizing looks at a passage and says, "The text says this, but it means this..." We want to avoid allegorizing Scripture as it separates meaning from the text. How do we guard against allegory as we seek to find Christ (or whatever your center is) in all of Scripture?

4. CREATION
or WHY PEOPLE LOVE COOKIE MUSH, THE ZIPLINE, SUNSETS, & FRIENDS

"Who has measured the waters in the hollow of his hand and marked off the heavens with a span, enclosed the dust of the earth in a measure and weighed the mountains in scales and the hills in a balance?"

- Isaiah 40:12

As we start to look at the main plot movements in the story of Scripture, I hope that you will see how each of the main plot movements are relevant to the whole story and is ultimately understood *in* and *through* Jesus.

The first main plot movement is that of Creation. We find the Creation story, and a kind of poem, of God making everything in the first two chapters of Genesis. It can be helpful to view Genesis 1-2 as three tellings of the same story. The first occurs in 1:1, and then you rewind, zoom in,[120] and get a closer look in 1:2-2:3 of 1:1. Then you rewind a touch, zoom in,[121] and get a closer look in 2:4-25 of 1:26-30. If that does not make sense to you, or you disagree, that is fine. Read it and you'll still get the message.

Pay attention to God's assessment of his creation and any variations in those assessments as he progresses.

---

[120] "Enhance!" – any episode of 24, probably.
[121] "Enhance!" – that joke is still funny to me.

Pray & Read: Genesis 1-2

1. What stands out to you in this story?

2. What does the story of creation reveal to you about who God is? List all the things that you can!

3. What does the story of creation reveal about who you are?

4. If man and woman are made in the image of God, what does that really mean? Experience shows us that we are not all-powerful and all-knowing beings. In what ways do we actually reflect God's image? In what ways are we like him? Can you support your answer biblically?

5. How does this passage testify to Christ?[122]

6. What does this passage mean for you as one who is *in Christ?*

7. What are you going to do in response? Who can you get to help you?

---

[122] Passages such as John 1:1-3 and Colossians 1:16 help us more fully understand the role of Jesus in creation. Thus, it is appropriate to read back the implications from those passages into Genesis 1-2. However, since that revelation about Jesus came later, it is worth it to first see how the passage testifies to Jesus within itself before reading back later texts into it. Read it and draw conclusions in its textual and epochal context before moving onto a canonical reading.

FOR FURTHER STUDY

Something to Read

There are five points that I want us to see. Five observations that I want to make sure inform our understanding of this first main part, this first plot movement, of Scripture. Five observations then we will talk about what this means for us and we will be done. This is a shorter lesson, so take your time!

First, God is Lord over all. God made everything. As Creator, He has authority over all His creation. Right from the beginning of Scripture we see that everything we have, everything we experience, and all that we know is from God. He made it so he gets to be in charge of it. In the winter of 2016-2017 I made a rowboat. It took me awhile and it was not particularly easy for me. Since I made it, it's mine. I get to decide who uses it and what happens with it. In an even bigger and more meaningful sense, God made everything so He gets to be in charge. He gets to be Lord over everything.

Second, the world was created good. This is important because it explains why there are good things in the world. The Bible tells us that God is good and He made the world to reflect His goodness. It reflects who He is. You can look at my boat and tell some things about me. You can tell that I like making things. You can tell that I cared about having a boat that would float and be functional. You can also tell that I got a little rushed. You can tell that I care a little bit about beauty, but also that I don't always pay as much attention to detail as I could. My boat reflects what kind of builder I am. It reflects what kind of person I am. In the same way, God is good and that is reflected in His creation.

The fact that God made the world good explains why we see good things in the world. It explains why we experience beauty and pleasure and joy in this world. The reason why people stop in the middle of the field to look at a sunset is because God made the world good and beautiful. The reason a boy will pick flowers for a girl is because God made a world in which things are good and beautiful. The reason that God made food taste good or music move us is because God created the world good. The reason why it is relaxing to sit in a swaying hammock and feel a cool breeze and hear the waves lapping against the bulkhead is because God made the world God.

Scripture again and again speaks to the way in which creation testifies to who God is.[123] There are truths about God to be seen in nature and we do well to make an effort to grow in our appreciation of the truths revealed in nature.[124]

The world was created good.

Third, God made us in his image.[125] There are all sorts of implications from this. Man and woman have intrinsic value. There is a to-the-core-significance about being made in God's image. All of creation reflects God, just as my rowboat reflects me. But only

---

[123] Psalm 19:1-6; Romans 1:19-20.
[124] As discussed in the section on the importance of Scripture, the special revelation of God's word guides our understanding of general revelation (what we can know about God through the Creation and our experience of it).
[125] You may hear this referred to as the *imago Dei*.

man and woman are made *in* God's image. [126] This means that the life of a person is worth something particularly significant. The lives of all people no matter their race, no matter their age, no matter their circumstances are valuable.

Being made in the image of God explains why we think and speak and act, because God is one who thinks and speaks and acts. There are all kinds of parallels. Let us consider an important one.

Is God ever alone? Before Genesis 1:1, was God alone? No, he is three in one. He is Father and Son and Holy Spirit. God is in perfect community.[127] It's a mystery how it works, but people were made for community, and friendship, and love as a reflection of the God who exists perfect fellowship as Father, Son, and Holy Spirit. God says in 2:18 that "it is not good for man to be alone. People were made to be together. That is why it feels good to have friends. That is why we don't like to always be alone.[128] We may want some alone time, but no one wants to be always alone, always unknown, always unloved. We were made in the image of God.

Fourth, people are to be fruitful and multiply and exercise dominion over the earth. In the account of Creation we see God placing man and woman in a good and fruitful land. He set them up to take care of things. The world is meant to be the place where people live their lives and we were meant to rule as

---

[126] This is why you sometimes hear mankind referred to as the 'crown of creation.'
[127] A unity that has only once been broken. Matthew 27:46.
[128] And thus solitary confinement is a terrible punishment.

regent kings and queens of the Emperor-King. In the Garden of Eden we see a harmony and peace in the created order. God placed people at the top of that order. You were meant to take care of the world around you. That is why people care about taking care of the world. That explains why people want to have a yard with nicely cut grass. It explains why people care about planting a garden or flowers. It explains why people desire to have a good living space.[129] It is why we ought to care about the environment, culture, and the world he has entrusted to us.

We were also supposed to reproduce. This explains why people want to have kids. It explains why God made sex to be so desirable. It was all a part of His plan.

Fifth, and the final thing I want us to notice as we look at Creation is that **there was a command to be obedient.**

Look at Genesis 2:16-17. From the beginning there was a demand to live a good life. Obedience meant a life knowing only goodness. Disobedience meant a life that has knowledge through the experience of both good and evil. There was a promised blessing for obedience and a promised curse for disobedience. We will continue to see this as we go through Scripture. There is a blessing for obedience and a curse for disobedience.

So what does this all mean for us?

---

[129] Any activity of culture-making can find it's origin in God's command to Adam in Eden.

Creation gives us a picture of one aspect of God's relationship to the world. He made it. He is Lord over it. He is right to be responsible for it. What He thinks about it matters. What He says brings life and blessing gets to be what brings life and blessing. And it's not all arbitrary, it reflects who He is.

Creation gives us a picture of what our relationship to God and the world was meant to be. We were supposed to all be at perfect peace and harmony. Everything was supposed to be good. Good with God. Good with people. Good with animals and nature. When we care about these things, we align with the purpose given to us in Eden.

Creation explains why pleasure and delight can be found in the world around us. The Bible explains this for us. Most other worldviews and religions spend all their time explaining why there is so much evil in the world without any explanation of why there is so much truth and beauty and goodness in the world. The Bible has an explanation.

Finally, since Creation reflects God it can be kind of a second book that teaches us about Him. Psalm 19, much of the book of Proverbs talks all about the things we can learn about God from the world around us. Romans 1 tells us that we can see God's power and divine nature by looking at the world around us. Jesus often uses analogies and metaphors from nature to teach truth. He will talk about a seed, or bearing fruit or foxes having dens. So also we can point to elements of the created order to illustrate spiritual truths.

The world can teach us some things about God and we do well to make an effort to grow in our appreciation of the truths in nature. I would encourage you to take time to appreciate the beauty of the world around you today. Slow down and look at the world around you and see how much good there is in it and thank God for making it so.

Some Related Scripture Passages:

Genesis 1-2

Job 38-40

Psalm 19

Psalm 104

Matthew 6:26-29

John 1:1-5

Colossians 1:16-17

Hebrews 1:1-4

Some Quotes:

"Recall once again the dilemma, 'if not a wise Providence, the a mere jumble of atoms,' and consider the profusion of evidence that this world is as it we a city…To those who insist, 'Where have you ever seen the gods, and how can you ne so assured of their existence, that you worship them in this way?' my answer is, 'For one thing, they are perfectly visible to the eye. For another, I have never seen my own soul either, but nonetheless do I venerate that. So it is with the gods; it is experience which proves their power every day, and therefore I am satisfied that they exist, and I do them reverence."[130] – Marcus Aurelius

"One touch of nature makes the whole world kin." – Shakespeare[131]

"Though I may not believe in the order of the universe, yet I love the sticky little leaves as they open in spring." – Fyodor Dostoevsky's Ivan Karamazov[132]

"I don't think it is enough appreciated how much an outdoor book the Bible is…It is best read and understood outdoors, and the farther outdoors the better." – Wendell Berry[133]

Questions for Further Reflection:

1. James said, "Religion that is pure and undefiled before God, the Father, is this: to visit orphans and widows in their affliction, and to keep yourself unstained from the world."[134] How does the story of Creation impact your view of orphans and widows?

2. Are the creation days actual 24-hour days? If so or if not, how do you know? How important is it to get this answer right? Why?

---

[130] Marcus Aurelius, *Meditations* (NY: Penguin Books, 2005), 4:3; 12:28.
[131] William Shakespeare, *Troilus & Cressida*, iii.3.
[132] Fyodor Dostoevsky, *The Brothers Karamazov*, trans. Constance Garnett (NY: Barnes & Noble Classics, 2004), 214.
[133] Wendell Berry, *Sex, Economy, Freedom & Community* (NY: Pantheon Books, 1993), 103.
[134] James 1:27.

3. Do you believe in a literal Adam and Eve? Why or why not? What are the implications either way?

5. THE FALL
or WHY WE HAVE RULES
or WHY I FIND IT HARD TO BELIEVE
IN A GOOD & LOVING FATHER

"None is righteous, no, not one;

No one understands;

No one seeks for God.

All have turned aside; together they have become worthless;

No one does good,

Not even one."

- Romans 3:10-12[135]

The second plot movement in the storyline of Scripture is the Fall. The fall of man came as a result of the disobedience that took place in Eden. The man and woman ate forbidden fruit from the tree of the knowledge of good and evil. In that moment man's relationship to everything changed as he turned his back on the God who is perfect goodness, perfect holiness, perfect truth, and perfect life.[136] That turn, that rebellion, has resulted in all of the evil, pain, and sorrow that we find in the world today.

---

[135] Or, Psalm 14:13; 53:1-3.
[136] And more… the giver of purpose, meaning, satisfaction, joy, delight, etc.

Pray & Read: Genesis 3

1. What stands out to you from this passage?

2. What can you learn from the way the serpent tempted Eve that will help you understand temptation? How did the serpent do it? Can you draw parallels to the temptations that you experience in your life?

3. What does the curse mean for the serpent? The woman? The man? Take your time here because you will see these elements of the curse over and over and over again throughout Scripture. Familiarity with them will help you recognize them when they show up so that you can connect later passages with what they mean in relation to the Fall.

4. Why does Adam's sin impact us? Is that fair?

5. How does this passage testify to Christ?

6. What does this passage mean for you as one who is *in Christ?*

7. What are you going to do in response? Who can you get to help you?

FOR FURTHER STUDY

Something to Read

The second plot movement in the storyline of Scripture is the Fall. When the man and woman ate the forbidden fruit from the tree of the knowledge of good and evil they rejected God's word, purpose for their lives, and a right relationship with him. In that moment man's relationship to everything changed. He turned his back on the God who is perfect goodness, perfect holiness, perfect truth, and perfect life. All of the evil, pain, and sorrow that we find in the world today finds its origin in that act. In this lesson, we will look at four observations from Genesis 3 and three implications that follow.

Observation #1: The temptation is familiar.

In Genesis 3:1-5, the serpent approaches the woman and asks, "Did God actually say, 'You shall not eat of any tree in the garden?'" and then later counters the woman's response with the statement, "You will not surely die. For God knows that when you eat of it your eyes will be opened, and you will be like God, knowing good and evil." He questions God's word, character, motives, and whether or not God truly knows what is best. We are likewise tempted to question God's word and to question if his way is really best.

Consider your greatest, or most common, temptation.[137] To choose to sin in that moment of temptation is to indicate that you believe you know a better way. That sin indicates a rejection of either that: (1) God has really said that action is a sin, or (2) God knows what is best for you and can be relied upon.[138] In Genesis 3 we see the original, and largely unchanged, formula for temptation.

Observation #2: Disobedience results in guilt, shame, and death.

We see the guilt and shame of Adam and Eve in two regards. First, they feel their nakedness. The idea here is not that nakedness is sinful, but that we feel exposed by our shame. Our guilt emanates outward from within so that we desire to be covered. Adam and Eve make an attempt to cover their guilt with fig leaves, but the covering is insufficient. Thus, and this is where we see our second example of their guilt and shame, they seek to hide themselves from God.

This makes it clear that their relationship with God has been broken. They were not made to hide from the

---

[137] Russell Moore suggests a 'desert island test' in his book *Tempted & Tried* (I give the book my highest recommendation). Imagine you are on a magical desert island where anything goes – there are no consequences and nothing is off limits. What would you do? Whatever your answer is to that question, that is probably an area of temptation that you need to be particularly guarded against.
[138] Again, I point you to Moore's *Tempted & Tried*. The book is a look at the temptations of Christ and how they are common to man. The first temptation is a temptation to trust the provision of the Lord (not just that God will feed me or give me a job, but that I can trust that he satisfies and will provide what I need). The second is a temptation towards vindication and the third is the temptation of a kingdom without a cross. All three have a root element of calling into question "has God really said?"

Lord in shame, yet they fled from his voice. We too may be tempted to run and hide from God. Admittedly, a part of that impulse is a reasonable response in our condition of sin. We recognize that our rebellion deserves death and judgment. However, in Christ, we know that he took our death and judgment in our place. We can instead run to him and confess our sins knowing that he is faithful and just to forgive us our sins.[139] Christ gives us a boldness that Adam and Eve could not reasonably have.[140]

I find it surprising, and I wonder if Adam and Eve felt the same way, that God did not give them the death that they deserved right away. Against expectation, the Lord in his mercy extends their lives in order that he may one day provide a means of deliverance and redemption. Their disobedience still results in death, but even in the just judgment of Genesis 3 we can see the Lord's mercy.

Observation #3: Evil messes up the good creation.

As a result of man's rebellion the Lord pronounces a curse. The curse has resulted in strained relationships, pain, and toil. The world was created good, but it is no longer *all* good and the Fall explains why we see both good and evil in the world around us.

Some of the language of Scripture goes as far as to make it sound like the creation now actually rebels against us as the insurrectionists. In Romans 8, the Spirit reveals that the whole of creation was, at the Fall,

---

[139] 1 John 1:9. He is faithful to do so, because he is gracious and loving and never fails. He is just, because our sin has been dealt with in Jesus. Thus, God is both just and the justifier (Romans 3:23-26).

[140] Hebrews 4:16.

placed under a bondage of decay and suffers and groans with longing for the day when things will be made right. The Fall explains tsunamis, hurricanes, terrorism, AIDS, black widows, road kill, cancer, and everything else in creation that causes pain and suffering.

Observation #4: We now live under a curse.

We see in the curse that the man and woman now have a broken and estranged relationship with God, with the creation, and with one another.

For the woman, the curse means pain in childbearing. Giving birth is a part of fulfilling God's plan to be fruitful and multiply.[141] Now it is an avenue of extreme physical pain that carries the possibility of emotional pain and, in too many cases, death. The Lord also states that there will be strife and disunity between man and woman. Human relationships are broken and no longer look the way that they are supposed to look.

For the man, he will work and labor in a world with a cursed ground. His work will be marked by toil and difficulty rather than joy and satisfaction in fulfilling God's purpose. The provision of food will be difficult and death will come in the end.[142]

Implication #1: Things are not the way they are supposed to be.

---

[141] Genesis 1:28.

[142] Note that in Genesis 3:19 God says, "By the sweat of your face you shall eat bread." I wonder if Adam really know what bread was at that point. The use of the word bread should be startling to us and ought to help us pay more attention throughout Scripture when we see bread in the story (or see a lack of bread).

We should not be surprised that dissatisfaction, discontentment, frustration, anger, and depression are common experiences. This world is broken and mankind is living an existence that does not match what the experience of life is meant to be.

Implication #2: We are all to blame.

The problem with the world is sin and we are all sinners. The world is broken and we broke it.[143] Rebellion causes all the suffering we experience and I am one who rebels. We complain and become bitter over the wrong that we see, yet we commit wrong all the time. As Father Zossima recounts to us, "every one is really responsible to all men for all men and for everything."[144]

Implication #3: The Fall explains the evil we see and experience.

The Fall is significant because it explains everything that is wrong with the world. It explains guilt, shame, and death. It explains the origin of evil in this universe. It explains why there is physical, emotional, and spiritual pain. It is the reason why things are not the way they are supposed to be. On account of the Fall

---

[143] Sometimes when somebody is going through a tough situation, perhaps facing cancer or a death in the family, our reaction can be to come alongside them and say "I'm sorry." On the surface that can sound like an unusual consolation (and really, I think the main consolation is being present with them in a tough time), but when we think further about it, we have reason to be sorry. Death and cancer and hard things happen in the world because of sin and I am one who sins everyday. I have reason to be sorry.

[144] Dostoevsky, *The Brothers Karamazov*, 266.

there is strife in our relationships with other people. We also find that our relationship with God has been ruined.

In the summer of 2008, on my way to the MU,[145] a friend asked me a rather blunt question after spending a few minutes talking about some spiritual things. As he sat on the bench with a counselor outside of Southern 12, he asked me, "So what do you struggle with? What is it for you?" While there is more than one answer to that question, the one that I gave that night was the freshest on my mind. When things do not go my way, it is easy for me to quickly become very angry with God. I tend to become very cynical of God's promise to cause all things to work together for good. I challenged him asking, "What good is a good that doesn't feel good? You say you love me, but what good is a love that doesn't feel like love?" My problem, at times, with God is that His world is really messed up. His world hurts and I don't like that.

This sort of thinking is familiar to many people. Perhaps it is experienced in varying degrees of intensity, but I think it is a common human experience that life does not always feel good and we want someone to blame.[146] If God is sovereign, then it certainly seems easiest to blame Him for what happens to us. Why the evil and suffering? For a greater good? Was He not smart enough to figure out a way to accomplish the same good without all the pain?

Fyodor Dostoevsky's Ivan Karamazov asks:

> Imagine that you are creating a fabric of human destiny with the object of making men happy in

---

[145] MU = Mobile Unit, where the guys' camp staff at CWR are housed.
[146] Forgetting that we are ultimately to blame.

> the end, giving them peace and rest at last, but that it was essential and inevitable to torture to death only one tiny creature – that baby beating its breast with its fist, for instance – and to found that edifice on its unavenged tears, would you consent to be the architect on those conditions? Tell me, and tell me the truth.[147]

This is a good question and we live in a world in which we know far more than one baby who has suffered. Ivan is not the only one to ask this question. The presence of evil in the world is the **one** decent argument against God. If you pay attention to what atheists say, it is the root argument that they have against a good and all-powerful God. I think we fool ourselves if we do not acknowledge that we can understand at least a little bit of where they are coming from. So how do we answer that question for ourselves and for others?

What Scripture says about creation and the Fall is an important part of how one deals with the issue of God and evil.[148] People have differing ways of saying why God allowed man to sin, but the key point of Scripture is that man sinned. Man was placed in a good world and he ate from the one tree that he was told to not eat from. Any answer to the question of evil that does not speak within the storyline of Scripture is going to be a deficient answer. The Christian answer to the question must include Scripture's account of creation and the Fall. If it does, it will naturally lead into the next part of the Story: Redemption. When the answer leads to a conversation about redemption in which the Gospel can then be presented. This is how we need to deal

---

[147] Dostoevsky, *The Brothers Karamazov*, 227. – read it, it's a Russian novel, so it is long, but it's worth it

[148] Arguments of theodicy seek to answer this question.

with these sorts of questions. We have to talk about the Gospel. It is the Spirit by the power of the Gospel that changes lives. Not arguments or answers to objections. Let us answer the objections, but may we do it in a way that leads to the Gospel.[149]

If you can talk about the storyline of Scripture then you have a ready defense for those who question why you believe what you believe. I think it is the best way to think through and respond to challenges like that from Ivan Karamazov. It has proven to me to be helpful in wrestling with personal hurt and disappointment. Yes, there is evil in the world. Man has a hand in that evil. If God were to get rid of evil today then those who have not been redeemed by the blood of the Lamb would face His wrath. That day will come. There will not always be evil, but He tarries. He waits so that more may come in. In the meantime, when faced with questions about pain, suffering, and evil – whether those questions come from others or our own hearts – the Fall gives us an explanation.

Some Related Scripture Passages:

Genesis 3-4

Job 21

Ecclesiastes 2:18-26; 3:16-22; 4; 9:1-6

---

[149] People don't reject God for intellectual reasons. They might hide behind intellectual objections, but the issue is an issue of the heart. I think this is the point of Psalm 14:1. Denial of God comes from a heart that is opposed to Him. It is a heart that is suppressing the truth that is clearly visible in the world around us. That heart is changed by the Gospel for it "is the power of God to salvation for everyone who believes."

Isaiah 6:8-13

Matthew 4:1-11

Romans 1:8-32; 5:12-21; 8:18-25

2 Corinthians 11:1-15

Revelation 12

Some Quotes:

"'Well, my dear Pangloss,' Candide said to them, 'when you were hanged, dissected, whipped, and tugging at the oar, did you continue to think that everything in this world happens for the best?'"
- Voltaire in *Candide*[150]

"It is then indeed meet for us to consider what a dreadful curse we have deserved, since all created things in themselves blameless, both on earth and in the visible heaven, undergo punishment for our sins; for it has not happened through their own fault, that they are liable to corruption. Thus the condemnation of mankind is imprinted on the heavens, and on the earth, and on all creatures."– John Calvin[151]

"So saying, her rash hand in evil hour
Forth reaching to the fruit, she plucked, she ate:
Earth felt the wound, and Nature from her seat
Sighing through all her works gave signs of woe,
That all was lost. Back to the thickest slunk."

---

[150] Voltaire, *Candide*, trans. Henry Morley (NY: Barnes & Noble Classics, 2003), 123.
[151] John Calvin, *Commentary on Romans*, 8:21.

"...With liberal hand: he scrupled not to eat
Against his better knowledge, not deceived,
But fondly overcome with female charm.
Earth trembled from her entrails, as again
In pangs, and Nature gave a second groan;
Sky loured, and muttering thunder, some sad drops
Wept at completing of the mortal sin
Original; wile Adam took no thought..."
- John Milton[152]

"How tides control the sea, and what becomes of me
How little things can slip out of your hands
How often people change, not to remain the same
Why things don't always turn out as you plan

These are things that I don't understand
Yeah, these are things that I don't understand

I can't, and I can't decide
Wrong, oh my wrong from right
Day, oh my day from night
Dark, oh my dark from light
I live, but I love this life"
Coldplay in "Things I Don't Understand"

Questions for Further Reflection:

1. If someone were to ask you why God would let the Fall happen, how would you answer? Could you give biblical support for your answer?

---

[152] John Milton, *Paradise Lost* (NY: Penguin Books, 2000), 205-206, IX.780.

2. Does the event of the Fall reveal that God's creation was imperfect or flawed?

3. What do you make of the lack of an explanation for the serpent's back-story?

6. REDEMPTION, PT. 1
or REDEMPTION PROMISED

"The LORD God said to the serpent...
'I will put enmity between you and the woman,
*and between your offspring and **her offspring**;*
*he shall bruise **your head**, and you shall bruise **his heel**.'"*
Genesis 3:14-15

-

We have covered Creation and have seen that it
explains everything good, true, beautiful, and real in
the world. We see that in the Fall we rebelled against
that. Genesis 3 gives us an explanation of everything
evil, false, ugly, and fake in the world.

In the third plot movement we see Redemption. This
will be broken up into two parts: redemption promised
and redemption begins.[153] Arguably you could take
everything from Genesis 3:15 until the NT (or more
specifically, the resurrection) as falling under the
category of redemption promised. Everything after
that in the NT rounds out the fulfillment of
redemption.

---

[153] There is actually a third part of redemption, redemption fully
realized (consummated), but that is actually the fourth plot
movement: New Creation.

Pray & Read (pick any combination!): Genesis 12:1-3; 15; Exodus 19:1-6; Deuteronomy 28:1-14; 2 Samuel 7; Psalm 2; 22; 89; 132; Isaiah 49:1-7; Jeremiah 30-33; Ezekiel 36:22-37:28

1. What stands out to you from these passages?

2. What conditions do you see in God's promises for redemption/deliverance/restoration?

3. Do you see anything indicating that God's promises of redemption, though conditional, are certain? If so, what? If not, what implication does that carry?

4. What longings for redemption do you see in our culture? In your family and circles of friends? In your own heart?

5. How do these passages testify to Christ?

6. What do these passages mean for you as one who is *in Christ*?

7. What are you going to do in response? Who can you get to help you?

FOR FURTHER STUDY

Something to Read

We want redemption. We want things to be made right and we know this inherently, deep down. It's built into us because we know that the world isn't the way it is supposed to be. If you look at our movies and stories you see that we are a people who desire a happy ending. We want things to turn out a certain way – the good guys win, the princes rescue the princesses, and everyone lives happily ever after. If you have ever seen a movie or read a story with a dark or unhappy ending you know that it does not sit well with us. You go away from the experience not feeling very good. It's because deep down we want to believe that things will be made right one day.

We want sick people to get well. We want estranged friendships to be restored. We want hard work to be easy. We hope that our 'last goodbye' with that friend or loved one really is not the last time we see them.

When we are having a great time we feel as though that time is going by too quickly; as though it is slipping out of our hands. We want the good times to last forever. When we are having a miserable time we want it to be over soon. But often feel as though the experience drags on.

All these emotions reveal that there is a desire within us to experience goodness forever instead of the challenges and misery and brokenness that we now face. We want redemption.

In Scripture we see the promise of redemption. The first three chapters of the Bible primarily focus on Creation and the Fall and the remaining 1,186 chapters deal with, in some way or another, Redemption. It's the third part of our storyline of Scripture.

We have the first promise,[154] the first glimpse of
redemption, in Genesis 3:15 as the LORD God says to
the serpent, "I will put enmity between you and the
woman, and between your offspring and her offspring;
he shall bruise your head, and you shall bruise his
heel."[155] There is not a whole lot of reason to expect
that Adam and Eve would have known quite what this
meant. Believers today still differ a bit on what exactly
it means. We can agree that all the promises of God
find their 'yes' in Jesus[156] and we can probably all agree
that a head bruising sounds worse, and more like a
possible mortal injury, than a heel bruising.[157] So I
think we can also reasonably conclude that Adam and
Eve would have been looking for big things out of any
future offspring.

In Genesis 3:20 we see that Adam believes the promise
as he calls the woman Eve, the 'mother of all living.'
It's a strange name to apply to someone who has just

---

[154] Theologians like to call this the *proto-euangelion* which is Greek
for the 'first good news.'

[155] The Hebrew term for 'seed' (also translated 'offspring') is a word
that is, as in English, both singular and collective. Thus the promise
could be pointing to one person, to one people, or to both. I believe
all three interpretations are consistent with seeing this text as being
a promise about Jesus. Jesus is an individual, but there is also 'a
people' – the church – that is *in* him. We see this in other places in
Scripture. For instance, in 2 Samuel 7, God promises David that one
of his sons will have the throne of his kingdom established forever
(2 Samuel 7:13), but Psalm 132 makes this promise sound like it will
apply to both one son and also many. It is hard to make sense of
this promise until we find out Jesus is the promised Son and that he
as a people *in* him who are co-heirs with him – at which point it is
evident how both promises can be true. I think we have a similar
thing going on in Genesis 3.

[156] 2 Corinthians 1:20.

[157] Though I would hate to get bit on the help by a snake!

earned death, but it is a reflection that Adam believes the promise that death will be delayed and that there is a promised seed to be on the look out for.

From there, in the Old Testament we see God reveal more and more about who this promised seed, this promised Son is, but there is something else going on too. We see the devil, the serpent, trying to stop him. Revelation 12 describes the story of the world as being that of the dragon chasing a pregnant woman and trying to snatch up her son at birth.[158] We see that imagery played out throughout the Old Testament. In the Old Testament we see the story of Christ[159] as God shows us: (1) our need for the Son, (2) people that look like decent options for a time but then come up short, and (3) how the devil tried to prevent the Son of a woman from coming.[160]

Consider Genesis 4 in light of the promise in Genesis 3. Redemption is promised to come through one born to a woman. What does the devil do in response? He eliminates the first two candidates as options to be the seed. Abel was murdered and Cain is cursed.

---

[158] If you accept that interpretation of Revelation. It makes sense to me! I like the explanation that Revelation, for the most part, tells the same story seven times from different angles/visions/images.

[159] This concept, that the point of the Old Testament is the story of the coming son, is not the only point to be found in the Old Testament. Many people would argue that it is not even the main point. Many others would argue that there is not even a main point, but maybe just a collection of good points. However, I feel that this is pretty close to the main point, if not the main point.

[160] The Old Testament only occasionally ascribes to the devil the wicked schemes it describes, but the New Testament provides this commentary for us.

If you continue on to the next chapter of Genesis, Lamech believes that Noah was the one who would bring "relief from our work and from the painful toil of our hands."[161] Then we see a corruption and wickedness of the human race that leads to the cataclysmic judgment of the Flood in Genesis 6-8. The Flood is a means of preserving Noah and God's promise of a deliverer.[162]

This continues throughout the Old Testament. Think about some of the stories that may be familiar to you if you grew up in the church. Just as soon as God reveals a little more information about the promised seed that would redeem, we see a devilish event that can easily be interpreted as an event to try to prevent the coming of the promised one:

-   *A promised one will come through Abraham and Sarah?*[163] Then let Pharaoh[164] take Sarah from Abraham, or let Abraham have a son by Hagar instead of Sarah.[165]

-   *He will come through Abraham and Sarah in the next year?* Then may King Abimelech try to take Sarah as a wife in the next 6 months. [166]

-   He will come through Isaac's son Jacob? [167]Then may Esau try to kill Jacob.[168]

---

[161] Genesis 5:29.
[162] Check out the New Testament commentary on these events in 1 Peter 3:18-22; 2 Peter 2:4-10; and possibly, Jude 5-7.
[163] Genesis 12:1-4; see also Genesis 15.
[164] Genesis 12.
[165] Genesis 16.
[166] Genesis 20.

- *He will come through the people of Israel?*[169] Then may they be enslaved and murdered by pharaoh.[170]

- If they are delivered from Egypt and declared to be the chosen people through whom redemption will come,[171] then may they turn from Yahweh and worship the calf.[172]

- If the people through whom he will be born are to live in the Promised Land,[173] then may the people be too afraid to ever enter that land.[174]

---

[167] Perhaps a hint of this in Genesis 25:23 and 27:27-29, but we see it a little more strongly in Genesis 35. If you are the devil, and you are paying attention, I think you are concerned about Jacob receiving a continuation of Abraham's blessing and assume these promises indicate he is the chosen line. That's a lot of assuming, and it is not spelled out explicitly in the text (which is the surest way to know), but it seems like a reasonable assessment.

[168] Genesis 27:41-42; 32:1-32.

[169] Genesis 35:1-15; Exodus 1:7; Exodus 4:22-23 uses language of God identifying Israel as his son. There is a lot of theological significance in this statement and some of that significance ends up connecting sonship with the promises of the Messiah (promised one/seed).

[170] Exodus 1:8-22. I don't think it matters that Pharaoh did not see his act as fulfilling a scheme of the devil, in the same way that I do not think Herod thought he was helping Satan out a few thousand years later when he ordered the same thing (Matthew 2:16-18). But both actions fit the image of Revelation 12 and it is not hard to believe that man's wicked desires may also align with the devil's schemes.

[171] Exodus 19:1-6. If they are a kingdom of priests, then they play a role as mediator between God and the nations. They would be an avenue of access to a restored relationship with the Lord. They mostly failed in this capacity until Jesus came to fulfill the promise (which he is still in the process of completing through his people).

[172] Exodus 32; also check out Stephen's commentary in Acts 7:39.

[173] Number 13:2.

[174] Numbers 13:25-14:12.

- *If He is to come through the line of King David,*[175] then may David be a murderer and an adulterer deserving of the death penalty.[176]

- *If He is to be the son of David,*[177] then may David's sons fight and kill one another for the Kingdom.[178]

- *If He is to come through Israel and the tribe of Judah,*[179] then may they be annihilated by foreign powers and assimilated into alien peoples as the Assyrians, and the Babylonians, and then the Macedonians, and then the Romans invade and conquer.

And on and on and on… the devil has sought to prevent the promised seed from coming.[180] And again and again God delivers in remarkable ways as he reveals more about *what kind* of son to look for.

As we learn more about who is to come and bring redemption, we see certain themes emerge. Some of the themes are almost hard to make sense of and seem contradictory and they end up really only making sense in Jesus Christ.

---

[175] 2 Samuel 7:8-16.
[176] 2 Samuel 11.
[177] 2 Samuel 7; Psalm 132.
[178] 2 Samuel 13-18; 1 Kings 1.
[179] Earliest Judah-specific promise in Genesis 49:10.
[180] Revelation 12 puts the devil as the one at work behind the scenes, but do not think that man was innocent throughout the story of the Old Testament. Man again and again fails to obey God and submit to his will. The efforts of the devil are executed by the actions of men.

REDEMPTION IS DEPENDENT ON THE OBEDIENCE OF MAN[181]

We are looking for one who would obey. The Old Testament is full of commands and full of stories of people who are incapable of keeping them. Psalm 132 is one of many examples where we see this at work. The psalmist explains that the covenant with David is dependent on an obedient son when he quotes the Lord as saying "One of the sons of your body I will set on your throne. If your sons keep my covenant and my testimonies that I shall teach them."[182] There needs to be a son who keeps all of God's commands.

EVEN THOUGH MEN CONTINUE TO FAIL, GOD PROMISES TO STILL DELIVER ON HIS PROMISES

He promises to come through. Over and over again He says He will provide what is needed. This is held in tension with the requirement for an obedient man. Look back at Psalm 132:11, "The LORD swore to David a sure oath." God made the promise and it is certain.

Throughout the Old Testament we are reminded that BLESSINGS ACCOMPANY OBEDIENCE AND CURSES AND DEATH ACCOMPANY DISOBEDIENCE. Read Deuteronomy 27-30 for a dramatic affirmation of this truth.

---

[181] This is easily, and often was, misunderstood as a works-based salvation. It ends up not being that because, the man Jesus (who is also God) ends up doing the work.
[182] Psalm 132:11-12.

83

WE KEEP HEARING ABOUT A PROMISED LAND
AND KINGDOM. We had Eden but were kicked out.
God then promises a restoration to a special land as he

Promise to:[183]	Obedience of Man Required	God will take care of it	Blessings & Curses	Promised Land & Kingdom
Noah	Gen. 6:14-22; 8:20-9:17[184]	Gen. 8:21[185]	Gen 9:3, 6	Gen. 9:1-3
Abraham	Genesis 12:1[186]	Gen. 15:12-17[187]	Gen. 12:2-3	Gen. 12:1; 15:7; 17:6; Rom. 4:1
Israel	Ex. 19-24; Deut. 30:11-20	Deut. 30:1-10[188]	Gen. 28:1-14, 15-68[189]	Deut. 17:14-20; 30:5
David	Psalm 132:11-12	Psalm 132:11-12	2 Sam. 7:14; Psalm 132:11-12	Ps. 2:8; 7:13; 72:8; 89:3-4, 28-37

---

[183] I have used Noah, Abraham, Israel, and David in this table. You could use Adam & Eve, Noah, Abraham, Isaac, Jacob, Israel right after the departure from Egypt, Israel right before entering Canaan, David, Solomon, a number of the prophets, Judah in exile, the returned exiles, and perhaps others that I have not thought of!
[184] In this particular passage, redemption is not necessarily seen to be dependent upon man's obedience, however it is seen that obedience is demanded.
[185] God made his promise to Noah and demanded obedience even though he acknowledges that man is evil to his core (Genesis 6:5-6).
[186] Abram had to leave his home and country and have a son (which required a little obedient activity on his part).
[187] God represents both parties in his covenant with Abraham while Abraham sleeps.

84

promises a kingdom for his people. Eventually he promises to include the whole earth in the redemption.[190]

When reading the Old Testament, we see that the saints of old are in eager anticipation as they wonder at how God might accomplish his promises.[191] It is important for us to understand that God was preparing the way for Christ and preserving the means by which he would come until the right time. Everything that happened in the Old Testament was a part of God's plan and leads up to the exact right moment when Jesus was to come.[192] In the Old Testament redemption through the Messiah, who turns out to be Jesus, is promised, foretold, and foreshadowed through words, people, and events. Understanding this is a big step in understanding how the Old Testament fits into the storyline of Scripture.[193]

---

[188] The Lord promises that even if Israel experiences the curse they will still receive the blessing.

[189] Exodus, Leviticus, Numbers, and Deuteronomy are full of examples!

[190] We see that easily in places like Psalm 2 and Isaiah 11, but Paul later tells us that this promise was even given to Abraham (Romans 4:13).

[191] Matthew 13:17; Luke 10:24; 1 Peter 1:10-12.

[192] Ephesians 1:10.

[193] Again, even if you do not see this as the main point of the Old Testament, perhaps you can still accept it as a thread throughout it. Scripture is rich and full of depth and this arguable should at least be a layer in your understanding of the Old Testament even if not *the main* layer.

Some Related Scripture Passages:

Genesis 12, 15, 17

Exodus 12-14, 19-24

Deuteronomy 27-30

2 Samuel 7

Psalm 2, 22, 89. 132

Isaiah 40-66

Jeremiah 30-33 (especially 31)

Ezekiel 36-37

Some Quotes:

"Here's the reason there are so many pages between the problem and the solution: God is providing for our instruction, endurance, encouragement, and, ultimately, our hope. As we see how God unfolds his glorious plan of redemption in Christ and how he keeps all of his promises, we learn to trust, love, and obey him. The Bible is so long and layered for a reason. It prepares us to see and receive Jesus as the only solution to our problem and the only Savior from our sin." – Trent Hunter[194]

---

[194] Trent Hunter and Stephen Wellum, *Christ from Beginning to End" How the Full Storu of Scripture Reveals the Full Glory of Christ* (Grand Rapids, MI: Zondervan, 2018), 100.

"It is vital that we understand the place given to certain key figures, such as Moses, in the Old Testament revelation. Their significance for us is not primarily in the way they stand as examples of godliness and faith, but rather in the role they play in revealing and foreshadowing the nature of the work of Christ." – Graeme Goldsworthy[195]

Questions for Further Reflection:

1. God spent a lot of time promising redemption. Why do you think it took so long for Him to bring it about? Or, more importantly, why does Scripture say it took so long?

2. What do you make of the Old Testament Law? Is it still applicable? If so, all of it or just parts of it? Do the Ten Commandments carry the same weight as regulations about what to do after a bodily discharge? Why or why not? If so, why is it that no one is upset that Leviticus 15 is not posted in county courthouses? If not, what is your basis for saying one is more important than the other? Can you support your answer with Scripture?

3. This particular study did not even touch on animal sacrifices in the OT. In what ways are there promises of redemption in the old system of animal sacrifices?

---

[195] Graeme Goldsworthy, *According to Plan: The Unfolding Revelation of God in the Bible* (Downers Grove, IL: IVP Academic), 132.

7. REDEMPTION, PT. 2
or REDEMPTION BEGINS

"From that time

Jesus began to preach, saying,

'Repent, for the kingdom of heaven is at hand.'"

Matthew 4:17[196]

This is the part of the storyline that is most clearly about Jesus. Redemption *comes through* Christ. It is *brought about by* Christ. It is *found in* Christ. The proclamation of the Gospel, the proclamation of the advancing kingdom of God, is the **proclamation of redemption in Jesus the promised Son of God**.

Pray & Read (again, pick any combination!): John 1:1-18; 3:14-21; Acts 7; Romans 1:1-4; Ephesians 1:3-10; Philippians 2:5-11; Colossians 1:13-20

1. What stands out to you from these passages?

2. Look back at your answers to #2 & #3 in "CREATION." Which of those characteristics also describe Jesus as the one who is both God and man?

3. Look back at the conditions you listed in #2 of "REDEMPTION, PT. 1." In what ways does Jesus fulfill those conditions? Does he fulfill them all?

---

[196] These are the first recorded words of the public ministry of Jesus in Matthew.

4. Look back at your list on #3 of "THE FALL." In what ways does Jesus undo and reverse the negative things on this list?

5. How do these passages testify to Christ?

6. What do these passages mean for you as one who is *in Christ?*

7. What are you going to do in response? Who can you get to help you?

FOR FURTHER STUDY

Something to Read

Last time we looked at the promises of redemption in the Old Testament and identified some themes that emerge about God's promised redemption. God made magnificent promises and then one day a man appears in a remote part of Galilee, in the former Kingdom of Israel. A man who, according to the opening verses of the Gospel according to Matthew is "the son of David," and according to Mark is "the Son of God," and according to Luke is "the Son of the Most High" who "will be given the throne of His father David, and...will reign over the house of Jacob (Israel) forever."[197]

And this man, Jesus, walks and lives about 30 years quietly before he crashes on the scene with the opening

---

[197] Luke 1:32.

words of his ministry saying, "Repent for the Kingdom of Heaven is here."[198]

As he goes around he makes it clear that he is the promised Son and that he sees himself as fulfilling all of the promises of the Old Testament.[199] He demonstrates that he is the one who will undo the effects of the Fall and the curse and he shows what kind of kingdom he is establishing:

-   One where man's relationship with Creation is restored as he heals sickness and calms storms and walks on water and rides young donkeys that haven't been trained.

-   A kingdom where man does not eat bread by the sweat of his brow but as a result of the extravagant blessing of God.[200]

-   A kingdom where people are restored in right relationships with one another. Where a Zealot and a tax collector can both be his disciples and break bread together.

-   A kingdom where people are restored into a right relationship with God.

All of this happens, this redemption is made possible, because he is THE PROMISED SON, THE OBEDIENT MAN, WHO WILL MAKE UP FOR MAN'S FAILINGS by dying on the cross for our sins as a substitute in our place and DELIVER ON GOD'S PROMISES as proven by his resurrection. The BLESSINGS for his obedience

---

[198] Matthew 4:17.

[199] Matthew 5:17-18.

[200] It is not that Jesus was really good at miracles but miscalculated a little bit when there were leftovers (Matthew 12:20). He was teaching the disciples a lesson about the kingdom.

he offers to us while taking the CURSES for our disobedience. And he promises to also resurrect us and make us new and take us into a promised LAND and into HIS KINGDOM.

That renewal starts now. It starts in our hearts and works outward. Changing our actions and our attitudes. Changing our hearts and actions towards God. Changing our hearts and actions towards other people. Even changing our hearts and actions towards the world around us.

Let us trust the Son and proclaim the good news of his coming to those who have not yet trusted him. All of history was building to His arrival. Even now, each passing day, each passing year, each passing decade is to give others the chance to trust Him. He will return one day and finish the work of making things right, but He has already begun and continues that work in the hearts of those who repent and follow him.

Man's rebellion in the Fall incurred the just wrath of God. God, in His grace, has delayed taking care of the problem of evil caused by man. But now, through the cross, the problem is solved. In dying on the cross Christ appeased God's wrath, but also made possible His gracious offer of redemption. Reconciliation is now possible. When one places his faith in Christ he is trusting that God has taken care of sin and death and made it possible to belong to a new race of man. A race that comes from the second, and last, Adam (who is Christ).

There is a great deal that could be and has been written about the redemption found in Christ. My main purpose here is to make the point that redemption is found in Christ alone.[201] It is the salvation that He has made possible of which the prophets of old spoke. So, when one considers the storyline of Scripture it is important to see that the third plot movement, Redemption, is the part of the story about how Jesus saves fallen man from sin and death.

Promise to:	Obedience of Man Required	God will take care of it	Blessings & Curses	Promised Land & Kingdom
Noah	Gen. 6:14-22; 8:20-9:17	Gen. 8:21	Gen 9:3, 6	Gen. 9:1-3
Abraham	Genesis 12:1	Gen. 15:12-17	Gen. 12:2-3	Gen. 12:1; 15:7; 17:6; Rom. 4:1
Israel	Ex. 19-24; Deut. 30:11-20	Deut. 30:1-10	Gen. 28:1-14, 15-68	Deut. 17:14-20; 30:5
David	Psalm 132:11-12	Psalm 132:11-12	2 Sam. 7:14; Psalm 132:11-12	Ps. 2:8; 7:13; 72:8; 89:3-4, 28-37
Us![202] Through & In Jesus	Phil. 2:7-8; Col. 2:9; 1 Tim. 3:16;[203] Heb. 4:15	John 1:1-16; Col. 1:13-20	2 Cor. 5:21; Rom. 8:17; Eph. 1:3	Heb. 1:2; Rom. 8:17

---

[201] Acts 4:12.

The redemption made possible by Jesus is the redemption for which we long.[204] It has begun, but is not yet complete. The process is underway in our hearts as we become more like Christ and underway in the world as more people come to know Jesus. Thus we have been saved,[205] we are being saved,[206] and we will be saved[207] by faith in Jesus.

Some Related Scripture Passages:

John 17-20

Acts 2, 7

Romans 10

Ephesians 1-3

Hebrews 10

---

[202] This is not to overlook that redemption is cosmic in its scope (e.g. Romans 8:18-25), but we will look at that more in the next plot movement in the storyline of Scripture.

[203] These verses speak to the Incarnation of Jesus ('incarnation' = God taking on flesh, God becoming man). Jesus is also indicated to be fully human by his ancestry (Matthew 1; Luke 1), his birth (Luke 2; Galatians 4:4), childhood (Luke 2), and his experience of hunger, thirst, fatigue, and the full spectrum of human emotions (Luke 4; Matthew 4; Luke 7:36ff; John 4:1-42; 11). At Christ's baptism, the Father affirmed Christ's obedience and his sonship (Mark 1:11). Regarding his obedience, see also: 2 Corinthians 5:21; Hebrews 4:15

[204] It is also noteworthy that corresponding to Redemption, as it is found in Christ, is the beginnings of the next plot movement in the story: New Creation. With the coming of Christ came the inauguration (beginnings of) the Kingdom of God. More on this to come...

[205] Romans 8:24; Ephesians 2:5.

[206] 1 Corinthians 5:2; 2 Corinthians 3:18.

[207] Romans 10:9; 13:11; 1 Peter 1:15.

Some Quotes:

"For the cross destroyed the enmity of God towards man, brought about the reconciliation, made the earth Heaven, associated men with angels, pulled down the citadel of death, unstrung the force of the devil, extinguished the power of sin, delivered the world from error, brought back the truth, expelled the Demons, destroyed temples, overturned altars, suppressed the sacrificial offering, implanted virtue, founded the Churches. The cross is the will of the Father, the glory of the Son, the rejoicing of the Spirit, the boast of Paul, "for," he says, "God forbid that I should boast save in the cross of our Lord Jesus Christ." The cross is that which is brighter than the sun, more brilliant than the sunbeam: for when the sun is darkened then the cross shines brightly: and the sun is darkened not because it is extinguished, but because it is overpowered by the brilliancy of the cross. The cross has broken our bond, it has made the prison of death ineffectual, it is the demonstration of the love of God. "For God so loved the world that He gave His only-begotten Son, that every one who believes in Him should not perish." And again Paul says "If being enemies we were reconciled to God by the death of His Son." The cross is the impregnable wall, the invulnerable shield, the safeguard of the rich, the resource of the poor, the defence of those who are exposed to snares, the armour of those who are attacked, the means of suppressing passion, and of acquiring virtue, the wonderful and marvellous sign. "For this generation seeks after a sign: and no sign shall be given it save the sign of Jonas;" and again Paul says, "for the Jews ask for a sign and the Greeks seek wisdom, but we preach Christ crucified." The cross opened Paradise, it brought in the robber, it conducted into the kingdom of Heaven the race of man which was about to perish, and was not worthy even of earth. So

94

great are the benefits which have sprung and do spring from the cross."

– St. John Chrysostom[208]

Questions for Further Reflection:

1. Why did Jesus have to die for us to be redeemed? Why couldn't God just forgive us?

2. Why is redemption only for those who repent and believe?

3. What about the man on the island, or wherever, who lives a good life but never hears about Jesus?[209]

---

[208] John Chrysostom, "Against Marcionsists and Manicheans, on the Passage 'Father, If it be Possible,'" in *Nicene & Post-Nicene Fathers: Chrysostom – On the Priesthood, Ascetic Treatises, Select Homilies and Letters, Homilies on the Statutes*, vol. 9, trans. W. R. W. Stephens, ed. Philip Schaff (Peabody, MA: Hendrickson Publishers, 2012), 203.
[209] If you have not read Romans 10 recently, you may want to read it before answering this question. And don't forget about lessons from the second plot movement of Scripture!

8. NEW CREATION
or REDEMPTION PT. 3: REDEMPTION FULLY REALIZED
or WILL THERE BE SEX, WORK, CANDY, FIDO, OR WHATEVER ELSE IN HEAVEN AND WHY THAT QUESTION IS TOO SMALL

"But according to his promise we are waiting for

new heavens and a new earth

in which righteousness dwells."

- 2 Peter 3:13

G. K. Chesterton in *The Everlasting Man:* "On the third day the friends of Christ coming at day-break to the place found the grave empty and the stone rolled away. In varying ways they realized the new wonder; but even they hardly realized that the world had died in the night. What they were looking at was the first day of a new creation, with a new heaven and a new earth; and in a semblance of the gardener God walked again in the garden, in the cool not of the evening but the dawn."[210]

---

[210] Chesterton, *The Everlasting Man*, 213.

Pray & Read: Philippians 1:6; 2 Corinthians 5:17; Revelation 21-22

1. What stands out to you from these passages?

2. According to these passages, when you die and go to heaven will you remain *there* forever?

3. According to these passages, what is the scope of the fulfillment of redemption? In other words, who and/or what is impacted?

4. From these passages, which promises of redemption have you not yet experienced?

5. How do these passages testify to Christ?

6. What do these passages mean for you as one who is *in Christ?*

7. What are you going to do in response? Who can you get to help you?

FOR FURTHER STUDY

Something to Read

In the final plot movement of Scripture we have the fulfillment of redemption in the New Creation. The story of Scripture begins with Creation, then there is the Fall from the way things are supposed to be, and the remaining plot movements are all tied to the idea of Redemption: redemption promised, redemption begins, and redemption fully realized. The vision of the New Creation in Scripture is one of full restoration and reconciliation. God has promised that all that is seen shall be remade into something splendidly more glorious than it was even in the days of Eden.[211] We will look at seven glimpses of the glory to come, but first let us consider two main ideas: redemption made complete in our own lives and redemption made complete in the created universe.

First, we see the beginnings of the new creation in our own lives. The Spirit of Christ tells us through Paul that "if anyone is in Christ, he is a new creation."[212] The New Creation has been initiated in our hearts and lives. We are being saved and now experience the creative and restorative work of our God in part, but that redemption and sanctification will one day be made complete. Paul proclaims with confidence that he is "sure of this, that he who began a good work in you will bring it to completion at the day of Jesus Christ."[213] He is so sure that that this work will be finished that he even speaks about it as though it is practically a done deal.[214] Right now we are being made more and more

---

[211] Romans 8:19-23; 1 Corinthians 15:37-41.
[212] 2 Corinthians 5:17.
[213] Philippians 1:6.
[214] Romans 8:30.

into the image of Christ.[215] One day this work will be made complete and we will be made like him. What has begun in our heart, mind, and soul will extend to our body: "[Jesus] will transform our lowly body to be like his glorious body, by the power that enables him even to subject all things to himself."[216] As we see in Paul's epistles, so also John encourages us that what we currently experience will soon be made complete: "Beloved, we are God's children now, and what we will be has not yet appeared; but we know that when he appears we shall be like him because we shall see him as he is."[217] The work of sanctification, of being made holy, will be completed in glorification, being fully holy, when we see Jesus.[218] In that moment, we will fully experience the New Creation of ourselves, but that is not the complete experience of the New Creation for redemption does not end with us.

The second thing we see as we study the idea of the New Creation in Scripture is that **redemption is cosmic in its scope**. Jesus tells us that he is "making all things new."[219] We also know that Creation is waiting patiently, but with groaning and eager longing, for the time when it will be set free from its bondage to death and decay.[220] One day during my first year on full-

---

[215] Romans 8:28-29. We call this "sanctification." Saints of old once referred to is as "deification."

[216] Philippians 3:21. We call this "glorification."

[217] 1 John 3:2.

[218] We will no longer feel the pull or temptation of sin. Augustine famously identified four states of man. In Eden man is able to sin and able to not sin (*posse peccare, posse non peccare*). After the Fall, man is not able to not sin (*non posse non peccare*). Now, after the cross but before the full institution of the New Creation, we are able to not sin (*posse non peccare*). In the final New Creation, we are unable to sin (*non posse peccare*). You can read more about this from Augustine in his "Treatise on Correction and Grace XXXIII."

[219] Revelation 22:5.

[220] Romans 8:18-22.

time staff at Camp Willow Run, I walked over to the office from the baggage car where I was living. Gina, our Administrative Assistant, was struggling to get the front door open. She had several things she was trying to carry inside that she had to set down to unlock the door. As she attempted to gather all of her items back up in her arms I realized that she seemed to be a bit distraught. I got in the office just as she was setting all of her things down and when she turned around from the counter and I could see her face it was clear to me that she was upset about something. I did not have to ask for an explanation as she quickly informed me why she was distressed. On her way to work she ran over a squirrel in the camp driveway. The squirrel had darted one way and then darted the other, seemingly incapable of making up its mind. Unsure of its fate as she passed, Gina looked in the rearview mirror and saw in the road what she hoped was a stick. Not wanting to continue without a certainty that the squirrel had survived, she stopped to see what the object was in the middle of the road. Alas, it was the poor squirrel that she had just run over. Gina was upset, and as she asked that arrangements be made to remove it so that she would not have to see it, I was reminded of Scripture. I figured it could be appropriate to share, so I turned to her and said, "Gina, all of creation is groaning with longing, waiting for the revelation of the sons of God. One day, this won't happen anymore." That is part of the promise of the New Creation.

John has a vision of a day when heaven and earth will be reborn and merged together.[221] This New Creation will be even better than what we know and see now. It will feel more like home and more right and real than the world we currently experience. C. S. Lewis

---

[221] Revelation 21.

illustrates this feeling in *The Last Battle* as the characters experience the land of a new Narnia after the final battle. Lord Digory explains to Peter Pevensie that the Narnia of old "was only a shadow or copy…[and] as different as a real thing is from a shadow or as waking life is from a dream."[222] Revelation 21:1-4 pictures the fulfillment of what Jesus previewed throughout the Gospels. There will be no more sorrow or pain or hunger or death. Neither will there be any more separation from God. God will dwell among his people and we will spend eternity in this new creation. Everything will be made right. God will remove all that is broken and wicked in the world as he deals with sin and darkness. Every tribe, nation, and tongue will be present and the kings will bring the glory of the nations into that place.[223] It is the day when Gina will kill no more squirrels.

Since the New Creation is something that is not entirely different from what God has done and since God has "set eternity" in our hearts,[224] it is not surprising that we see some glimpses of the glory to come in the New Creation in our current experience. Let us take a look at a couple of these glimpses of glory.

Glimpse #1: Worship

I used to be a little bit afraid of heaven. It was not an admission I was proud of or wanted to openly share. I felt bad about it, but really I thought heaven sounded kind of boring. I understood that we would spend eternity worshiping God and it was so hard for me to envision how we could sing songs for a billion years and not get tired of the experience. A part of me still thinks I could get a little bored singing for that long,

---

[222] C. S. Lewis, *The Last Battle* (NY: HarperTrophy, 2000), 195.
[223] Revelation 5:9; 21:24-26.
[224] Ecclesiastes 3:11.

but I now recognize that there is still a part of my flesh that is being put to death that fails to see that God is worthy of a billion years of songs. A relationship with him is so satisfying that it would be pleasure forevermore.[225] I also now see that I had a view of worship that was too narrow and limited. Worship is not just that part of a church service when you sing songs. Nor is it only a type of music genre that I listen to when I want to focus on Jesus. The living of our lives is supposed to be an act of worship. Consider Romans 12:1, "I appeal to you therefore, brothers, by the mercies of God, to present your bodies as a living sacrifice, holy and acceptable to God, which is your spiritual worship." And look at Colossians 3:17. "And whatever you do, in word or deed, do everything in the name of the Lord Jesus, giving thanks to God the Father through him."[226]

An eternity of worship of God in the new creation is not just a large gathering of people singing songs, though it sounds like it may include that at times.[227] It is an eternity of living lives honoring and pleasing to God and in relationship with him. The process of living, working, playing, etc. as worship begins now as we live out Colossians 3:16-17, but it is something that we will one day experience to the full. So we must be careful to not have too narrow of an understanding of what eternity entails.

Glimpse #2: Seeds

We know that Christ loves to bring an abundance of life to his work, but we also have a remarkable image

---

[225] Psalm 16:11.
[226] See also Psalm 51:17.
[227] Revelation 7:9-12.

of new life in 1 Corinthians 15:35-49.[228] It is the image of the seed. We forget the miracle of the seed because it is so common to us. However, if you did not know anything about a seed you would never expect it to do what it does. You can take a seed that has been dormant in an envelope for a few years – dead by all appearances – put it in the dirt, and with the right conditions that unremarkable little grain will be transformed into something unexpected and unimaginable. If you did not know better you would never guess that a seed could become a rose bush or a corn stalk or a mighty oak tree. Scripture uses the experience of the seed to illustrate what will happen to us. We are that seed and we too will one day be placed in the earth and a most unexpected transformation will one day take place when the time and conditions are right. Except that the Spirit has told us something about the coming transformation, it will be so remarkable that would no more be able to guess at what the result will be anymore than we could have ever guessed that a rose bush, corn stalk, or oak would have come out of a seed. Such is the type of transformation and glory that will accompany the ushering in of the New Creation.

Glimpse #3: Eden

In Scripture, Eden gives us a glimpse of the New Creation. Eden is the old creation and provides a picture of the way things are meant to be. This may be obvious, but the description of the New Creation as a "New" Creation indicates some level of continuity with the old creation. There will be harmony and peace in the created order. There will be perfect stability in creation. Man will properly exercise dominion over the earth. The wolf shall dwell with the lamb and "the

---

[228] See John 10:10 and Matthew 15:37,

weaned child shall put his hand on the adder's den."[229]
The way things were supposed to be in Eden, the New
Creation will be at least as good. We will live in peace
with God, with others, and with the created order.

Glimpse #4: Jesus doing crazy stuff in the Gospels

Christ, in the Gospels, gives us another glimpse. He is
the perfect man and shows us what it looks like to
interact with God, people, and creation as a perfect
man. His miracles and acts point to a restoration to
how things are supposed to be and preview the
advancing Kingdom of God that will be made
complete in the New Creation. There will be a healing
of sickness and disease and we shall feast.[230] Christ
exerts control over creation as he calms the storm and
walks on water. Peter experiences something of the
coming day of the New Creation when he steps out of
the boat onto the waves. In that moment, Peter gets a
taste of what it will be like to see Jesus and be made
like him.[231] Christ, in his resurrected body, which we
will also one day share,[232] ate fish,[233] passed through
walls,[234] disappeared and reappeared, and flew.[235] All
of these things may be pictures of what is to come.[236]

---

[229] Isaiah 11:6-10.

[230] Matthew 14:13-21; Revelation 19:6-9

[231] 1 John 3:2.

[232] 1 Corinthians 15: 49; 1 John 3:2.

[233] Luke 24:42-43; also may be implied in John 21:9-15.

[234] John 20:19.

[235] Or maybe merely ascended. Acts 1:9.

[236] I am hesitant to say that every aspect of what Christ did will
characterize our experience of the New Creation because we do not
know for certain. These are guesses based off of glimpses. To see
the experience of the resurrected Jesus in the broken world through
our eyes as not-yet-glorified people is like looking through a
darkened glass (1 Corinthians 13:12). To might look back in a
thousand years on the excited exclamation that we may one day fly
like Jesus and compare it to a toddler's excitement to find out that
adults can have pacifiers whenever they want. It may be true, but

DWELL IN THE WORD

Glimpse #5: Time flies (or drags on)

Our experience of time gives us a glimpse. When things are going well, time seems to pass quickly and it feels as though it escapes us. This points to our innate desire to experience goodness without end. Conversely, when things are going poorly time seems to drag on. This points to our innate desire to experience only goodness. In the glory of the New Creation, the expression "time flies" will lose its meaning. We will never have to fearfully check our watches to see if we are out of time. We will never agonizingly glance at the clock and realize that we have to endure more boredom or pain for just a little while longer. One day we will experience the good of life without the worry of when it will end.

Glimpse #6: Work

This is speculative, as many of these glimpses are, but I think we will work in the new creation. In Eden people were meant to work even before the Fall. With the Fall came toil and hardship. Toil in labor, but not work itself, is a result of the curse. We even get glimpses of our desire to work here in this life. Work can be satisfying at times. Many people fear idleness, and those who prefer laziness are typically looked down upon. There is a general sense that work is a good thing – you just have to find what you enjoy. These experiences provide an idea of how things are supposed to be. We can work with joy and satisfaction. Furthermore, we see in Scripture that we will rule the created order and will even judge the angels.[237] It is also evident that the best aspects of every culture and

---

something of so little concern in light of all the better things that will define our experience.

[237] 2 Timothy 2:12; 1 Corinthians 6:3.

civilization will be represented in the New Creation.[238] Perhaps this indicates that culture-building will continue. While I am not sure exactly what this will look like, I do think that we will work in glory, but it will not be the sort of work that is described as toil or agony.

Glimpse #7: Pleasure & Contentment

Finally, I think any genuine pleasure that we experience is a glimpse of the glory to come in the new creation. I am often asked if there will be certain things or experiences in heaven, such as sex, or fishing, or Cheerwine, or dancing, etc. While I do think that there are some things that we can confidently say will be a part of eternity, since Scripture names a few things explicitly, I am reluctant to say specifically what the experience will be like. However, we can know that that whatever we do or have in the New Creation has to be at least as good as the best pleasure on earth. Will there be sex or candy in heaven? Whatever there is, it has to be at least as good as sex and candy. Will there be mountain climbing or wakeboarding in heaven? I am not sure, but it has to be at least as good as the rush of mountain climbing and wakeboarding. The pleasure of the new creation has to be at least as good as the pleasure derived from fishing, or Cheerwine, or dancing because we will not look back on our experience from before with longing since that which is to come is greater than that which currently is. Pleasure and contentment in things and experiences is a gift from God that we now only experience in part.[239] In the fully realized redemption of the New Creation we will experience complete pleasure and contentment in God. If that comes in things and experiences it will

---

[238] Revelation 21:24-26.
[239] Psalm 16:2; James 1:17.

be in the recognition that those things are *from* God. Ultimately our pleasure and contentment will come from being reconciled to God for all of eternity and that exceeds any other pleasure we may now think we desire.[240] St. Augustine prayed, "Thou hast made us for Thyself and our hearts are restless until they rest in Thee."[241] The experience of the New Creation will be of a perfect pleasure and contentment that comes from a true rest in God.

So, what does all this mean for us now? "But the day of the Lord will come like a thief, and then the heavens will pass away with a roar, and the elements will be burned up and dissolved, and the earth and the works that are done will be exposed. Since all these things are thus to be dissolved, what sort of people ought you to be in lives of holiness and godliness, waiting for and hastening the coming of the day of God, because of which the heavens will be set on fire and dissolved, and the elements will melt as they burn! But according to his promise we are waiting for new heavens and a new earth in which righteousness dwells."[242]

How do we hasten the day? We advance the Kingdom of God. We share the Gospel and see the Spirit set hearts on fire by the Word of God as people turn towards the Christ who calls us from death to life and from the old to the New Creation.[243]

---

[240] Though this is not a desire that will just one day show up in glory. If you do not currently desire the joy of a reconciled relationship with God, you will need to be born-again in order to be well-suited for the New Creation.
[241] Augustine, *Confessions,* 3.
[242] 2 Peter 3:10-13
[243] Luke 24:32

Some Related Scripture Passages:

Isaiah 11:6-9

Isaiah 60

Isaiah 65:17-25

Isaiah 66:22-23

Matthew 5:5

Mark 12:25-27

John 14:2-4

Romans 8:18-25

I Corinthians 6:3

I Corinthians 15:35-49

Hebrews 1:11-12

Hebrews 12:26-27

2 Peter 3:13

1 John 3:2

Revelation 21-22

Some Quotes:

"That powerless body shall be raised in power. That was a fine idea of Martin Luther, which he borrowed from Anselm, that the saints shall be so strong when they are risen from the dead, that if they chose they could shake the world; they could pull up islands by their roots, or hurl mountains into the air... I think if

we do not go the length of the poets, we have every
reason to believe that the power of the risen body will
be utterly inconceivable. These, however, are but
guesses at the truth; this great mystery is yet beyond us.
I believe that when I shall enter upon my new body, I
shall be able to fly from one spot to another, like a
thought, as swiftly as I will; I shall be here and there,
swift as the rays of light. From strength to strength, my
spirit shall be able to leap onward to obey the behests
of God; upborne with wings of ether, it shall flash its
way across the shoreless sea, and see the glory of God
in all his works, and yet ever behold his face. For the
eye shall then be strong enough to pierce through
leagues of distance, and the memory shall never fail.
The heart shall be able to love to a fiery degree, and the
head to comprehend right thoroughly"

- Charles Spurgeon in "Resurgam"

"He has forced open a door that has been locked since
the death of the first man. He has met, fought, and
beaten the King of Death. Everything is different
because He has done so. This is the beginning of the
New Creation: a new chapter in cosmic history has
opened."

- C. S. Lewis in Miracles[244]

"Every time we gather together to eat bread and drink
wine together, we hear Jesus announcing, 'Your
sensory appetites are real and good and created, and
they are pointing beyond themselves to something
beyond all you could ask for or even imagine.' The
Lord's Table, then, isn't just a visual aid to remind us,
as though it were a memory-jogging tool. As we gather

---

[244] C. S. Lewis, *Miracles* (NY: HarperCollinsPublishers, 1996), 237.

together around the Table, we are being trained to eat at the 'big table' in Jerusalem. And were announcing to ourselves, and to the satanic powers in the air around us, what's really true. 'Eat, drink, and be merry, for tomorrow we die' is a sham. The alternative is not a refusal to eat, drink or be merry. That would be ingratitude. **Instead, with the resurrected Jesus we sing out, 'Let us eat, drink, and be merry, for yesterday we were dead.'"**

- Russell D. Moore in Tempted and Tried (emphasis mine)[245]

Questions for Further Reflection:

1. In John 14, Jesus tells us that he is going to prepare a place for us. Why was it important to Jesus that he let us know that?

2. People believe lots of different things about what happens after death. Below are listed five views that are still prevalent today. How would you respond biblically to someone that holds one of these views? In what ways is the biblical view better? In what ways does the storyline of Scripture and the biblical idea of a New Creation better satisfy man's longings than the following:
- Annihilation (the idea that we cease to exist at death)

- Angelism (the idea that only our souls live forever)

---

[245] Russell D. Moore, *Tempted and Tried* (Wheaton, IL: Crossway, 2011), 75.

- Pantheism (the idea that we are reabsorbed into one divine being, in other words, we all just become one big god together)

- Ghosts (the idea that we exist in a sort of shadowy existence)

- Reincarnation (the idea that we will be born again into another life)

3. I have several times heard statements similar to this one: "We do not need to waste time thinking about what heaven will be like. We will all know one day, but no one knows yet, so no need to waste time speculating." Do you agree with this view? Why or why not? Can you support your view with Scripture?

9. DAVID, JONATHAN, AND THE IMPORTANCE OF FRIENDSHIP
or I AM: THE FRIEND & SO CAN YOU

"How the mighty have fallen in the midst of battle!

Jonathan lies slain on your high places.

*I am distressed for you **my brother Jonathan**;*

very pleasant have you been to me;

***your love to me** was extraordinary,*

surpassing the love of women."

David's lament in 2 Samuel 1:25-26

Friendship is important and is a reflection of the God-given desire we have for community. In this section we will look at one of the most famous friendships in Scripture: David and Jonathan.

Pray & Read: Psalm 16:1-3; 1 Samuel 18:1-5; 19:1-7; 20:1-42

1. What stands out to you in the story of David & Jonathan's friendship?

2. What characteristics and descriptions can you find regarding their friendship?

3. What characteristics of the friendship between David & Jonathan are familiar and present in your own friendships? Do any aspects seem strange and unfamiliar to you? How can you foster similar characteristics in your friendships today? This week? This year?

4. In Psalm 16:3 it seems like David is making an idol of fellowship with the saints and elevating friendship and people beyond their proper place as he declares that they are the ones "in whom is *all* my delight." Is David in the wrong here? If so, how do you maintain that Psalm 16:3 is God's inspired word?[246] If not, why not?

5. How does this passage testify to Christ?

6. What does this passage mean for you as one who is *in Christ?*

---

[246] There are some options here, but you would need to be careful that you do not wander into territory that allows you to too easily dismiss God's word as authoritative.

7. What are you going to do in response? Who can you get to help you?

FOR FURTHER STUDY

Something to Read

Friendships are important. Nobody really likes to be alone. We are made to have friends. Remember what Genesis said? We are made in God's image and God is never alone because he is three in one! God also says in Genesis 2:18 "it is not good" that man should be alone. Regarding everything else he says, "it is good" but then he says "it is not good" that man be alone. This was the only time in the creation story that he states that something is not good. So he makes another person, the woman, and then says "it is very good."

One of my favorite statements about friends comes from G. K. Chesterton: "It may be conceded to the mathematicians that four is twice two. But two is not twice one; two is two thousand times one."[247] He starts out talking about math, but finishes by talking about friends.

Friendships are important and the Bible says a lot about friends. In the story of David and Jonathan we see characteristics of a deep friendship that provide an excellent model to us.

Friends are knit together.

---

[247] G. K. Chesterton, *The Man Who Was Thursday.*

"The soul of Jonathan was knit to the soul of David."[248] They were brought together. Like someone else was intertwining, or knitting, their lives together. God was. If you consider your close friendships, you probably notice something similar. As you grow together as friends your lives intersect in various ways. You eat together, play together, and maybe work together. You share in one another's interests and pursuits. Your lives are defined by a degree of togetherness.

A less than obvious takeaway from this verse is to make friends wherever you are. Obviously you cannot easily make friends somewhere that you are not. So make friends where you are. God has placed people around you for a reason. Sometimes you have an instant friendship with someone while with others it may take time.

Some of my friends were pretty quick friends. I have this friend Zachary; the Lord knit us together pretty quickly. We have another friend Scott. One of my all-stars. We knew each other for probably about two years before we were real close

My point is that that knitting together does not always happen quickly. Just because you are not super close with a person now, does not mean you will not one day be close friends. So keep being a friend and make friends where you are and with the people in your life. God has placed them in your life for a reason and he has demonstrated that he likes to knit unexpected friends together.

---

[248] 1 Samuel 18:1.

115

Friends show one another love & selflessness & generosity.

"And Jonathan loved him as his own soul."[249] There is a selflessness evident here. Jonathan does not view himself as better than David. He loves David as he loves himself. It is similar to the idea to "do unto others what you would have them do unto you."[250]

Notice in 1 Samuel 18:4 that Jonathan gives David his robe and armor and sword. He gave him the shirt off his back! Friends like to be generous towards one another and like to care for one another. At times this may actually be giving material things. It is also giving time and attention. Checking in. Sending a note or message of encouragement.[251]

Friends delight in one another.

"Jonathan, Saul's son, delighted much in David."[252] Friends take delight in one another. Be cautious here that you do not take this to mean that it is okay to only attempt to be friends with people you like. Everyone has value and you should look to have friendships and delight with people that you may not initially think

---

[249] 1 Samuel 18:1.
[250] Luke 6:31.
[251] Often when I sit down to write someone a note of encouragement or a letter to let them know how much I admire them, I feel funny about it; a little strange and a little weird. I wonder how it will be received and can almost talk myself out of it. However, when I have received that kind of note or letter from a friend, I have never through it was weird or strange. Instead, I have kept those notes and letters as something dear and treasured to me. So don't be afraid to write your friends and show them some love!
[252] 1 Samuel 19:1.

DWELL IN THE WORD

you could like.[253] They are made by God and loved by God. If he can find a reason to delight in them, so can you!

I have a good friend, by the name of Harrison. First time I saw him, I was certain I wouldn't like him. I could tell that he was going to be an annoying, know-it-all, turn-your-nose-up 'Richmond guy.' Turns out I was wrong. He became a dear friend and my experience of life would be poorer had I not been in a situation where I had to befriend him. Delight in your friends.

Jonathan delights in David and David delights in his friends. These words come to us from David: "I say to the LORD, 'You are my Lord; I have no good apart from you.' As for the saints in the land, they are the excellent ones, in whom is all my delight."[254]

What a surprising thing to say! "All my delight." It sounds like a statement that you should only say about God. David is acknowledging that all the good he has in his life is a gift from God and here he is talking about how much his friends, the saints, mean to him.[255] He recognizes and praises God for the good gift of friends that he has received. It's good to have good friends!

Let's explore this further and go to kind of a weird verse. Go to Psalm 133. It's another psalm of David.

---

[253] It is also hard to imagine that you can love your neighbor (Mark 12:31) and your enemies (Matthew 5:44) without acting as a friend towards them. You may not end up being friends, but as much as it is up to you, be a friend to them (Romans 12:18).
[254] Psalm 16:2–3.
[255] David's statement is similar to what we see in James 1:17. We should recognize that every good thing we have comes from our Father God. When we know that it comes from him and we enjoy and delight in what he has given us, we honor him.

"Behold, how good and pleasant it is when brothers dwell in unity. It is like the precious oil on the head, running down on the beard, on the beard of Aaron, running down on the collar of his robes!"

Strange verse, right!? Did anyone today look around and say, "This is great. We're having a lot of fun. I love seeing everyone together like this. It's as good as seeing some oil run down a man's beard!"

That would be an unusual thing for us to say. David makes a comparison that is unfamiliar to us, but we can probably come close to understanding it with a little effort.

You likely know who Aaron is. He is the brother of Moses and the high priest for the people that was chosen and anointed by God. He is the head of the Israelite priesthood. Every man descending from him who was to serve as a priest was anointed, or marked, as chosen. The high priest was anointed on the head and it was a messy business. There was an overflow of oil; an extravagance of oil. Since the oil was special for what it signified it was a special moment and there was a special extravagance about it.

When people are together in unity. When they are friends, when they are brothers and sisters and family. There is an extravagance of God's blessing in it. It is something special.

If that's hard to follow, or all that seems like stretch to you, don't worry about it. The big point is this: friends are good and we should delight in our friends.

Friends speak well of one another.

"And Jonathan spoke well of David."[256] Talk up your friends. Be an advocate for them. Speak to their strengths. Build them up to their faces and behind their backs. It's what a friend does.

Friends look out for one another.

In chapter 20, Jonathan uncovers his father's plot to kill David. He warns David because he cares for and looks out for David – at the expense of a future kingdom. You again have selflessness on the part of Jonathan. King Saul views David as a competitor to the throne and Jonathan, the son of Saul, could have reasonably thought the same. Instead he seeks to care for and preserve David's life.

Look out for your friends. If they are in danger, get them the appropriate help. If you see them coming under attack – whether that be temptation towards sin, a sense of nagging shame, or heading towards a trap that the devil may have for them – speak up! Warn them! Share the truth, share God's word, encourage them, and be bold! David had a promise from God. A promise that we know was for salvation and a future kingdom.[257] Jonathan didn't stand in the way of that.[258] He sought to help and we can do the same. Be a friend who seeks to see God's salvation and kingdom worked out in the lives of your friends.

---

[256] 1 Samuel 19:4.

[257] 1 Samuel 16:1-13. David is anointed as the one chosen by the Lord to replace Saul. From the text it is not explicit that David knew that was the purpose to which he was chosen. Many commentaries suggest that he likely knew the significance of the anointing. However, it is not clear from the text alone. What is clear is that he would have known that he was chosen by the LORD as someone special and for a special purpose.

[258] Jonathan says as much in 1 Samuel 23:16-17.

Friends bear one another's burdens.

"And they kissed one another and wept with one another, David weeping the most."[259] The takeaway here is not to kiss you friends, but I suppose it could be.[260] Let us instead focus on the weeping part. Friends are sad together at sad moments.

This is the same idea we have in Romans 12:15, "Rejoice with those who rejoice, weep with those who weep." Support your friends in what they are feeling. If your friend is having a rough time take time to get with them and share in the feeling of the roughness of it. Acknowledge that it is rough and be with them.[261]

In all of this, Jonathan is bearing David's burden with him. This is an important part of friendship.

Friends want to be together, but value God's plan for each other most of all.

The other thing here, and you all know this if you have ever experienced it, is that friends will be sad to part. David and Jonathan are so close and they do not know if they will see one another again.[262]

---

[259] 1 Samuel 20:41.
[260] We should be affectionate with our friends. That may look different in various cultures, but the desire for affection is universal. Show your friends appropriate affection!
[261] In those moments, do not feel like you have to have the perfect thing to say. You probably do not have anything perfect to say anyway and even if you did they likely will not remember it. But they will remember that you were there. Be with your friends in times of sorrow and share with them in their grief.
[262] In Acts 20, we have another similar story. Paul has a sense he is setting out on a path that is going to lead to imprisonment and affliction. He sends for his Ephesian friends to see them one last

Friends are bonded together and sad to part ways. Maybe you have seen this already in your life. Maybe a friend has moved away or you moved or something along those lines. Maybe you have experienced the death of a friend and even now it stings to be separated from them. If you haven't experienced the parting of a friend, there is a good chance it is coming one day. And when you feel sad about it, that's okay. Friendship is a good gift from the Lord and it can be hard to part ways. Thankfully, parting ways isn't the same as the friendship ending.

In Christ, resurrection is coming. We will all be brought together again one day. When we are all back together, we will have the next 10,000 years and more to hang out, and play together, and work together, and worship God saying, "You are my LORD; I have no good apart from you! As for these saints in this land, in this new creation you have given us, they are the excellent ones, in whom is all my delight!"

In conclusion, we have a good example from Jonathan and David of what friendship should look like. Friends are:

- Knit together.

- Love one another, are selfless, and serve one another.

- Generous towards one another.

---

time. They talk, and then right before they part, they do the same thing we saw with Jonathan and David. They kiss and weep! They are sad to part ways. They want to stay together, but they value following God's plan above all.

- Delight in one another.

- Speak well of one another.

- Look out for one another.

- Bear one another burdens.

- Want to be together, but value God's plan for each other most of all.

Let us wrap it up by pointing it back to Christ. David's life matters because of how it related to Christ.[263] And Jesus, like in everything worth being good at, is the best at all this. He is the best at being a friend.[264]

- Knit together. - Jesus bonded himself to us. He left the glories and riches of heaven to become a man and tie his life to ours.

- Love one another, are selfless and serve one another. - Consider 1 John 3:16, "By this we know love, that [Jesus] laid down his life for us."

- Generous towards one another. - He held nothing back from us. He has given us the greatest thing he could give us: himself.

- Delight in one another. - Zephaniah 3:17 tells us that God delights in us. Hebrews 12:2 tells us that Jesus endured the cross because of the joy set before him. The joy was a redeemed and

---

[263] Jesus is both the shoot that springs up from the stump of David (Isaiah 6:13; 11:1; Matthew 21:9) and the root of David (Revelation 5:5). Jesus is David's life-source and his offspring. Meaning, remarkably, he is both the root and descendent of David (Revelation 22:16).
[264] And more!

restored people. You and me and all those that trust Him. He delights in us.

- Speak well of one another. Jesus speaks so well of you that he calls you a child of God and makes you into one.

- Look out for one another. - Christ made our salvation possible. He delivered us from the greatest dangers of all.

- Bear one another burdens. - All the burden of sin and shame and death, Christ bore that for us.

- Want to be together, but value God's plan for each other most of all. When Jesus left, He promised to return. He left as a part of God's plan that more might be saved, but He has not left us alone (he gave us his Spirit), nor for long.

Know that Jesus wants to be the best friend you have ever had and know that He is placing people in your lives that are meant to be your friends. You have felt both of these things before, I hope. Continue to be a friend to those that God has placed in your life. Be like David. Be like Jonathan. Be like Jesus.

Some Related Scripture Passages:

Psalm 133

Proverbs 17:17; 18:24; 27:5-6; 27:17;

Ecclesiastes 4:9-10

John 15:12-15

Romans 12:10-11

Colossians 3:12-15

Some Quotes:

"No one would choose to live without friends even if he had all the other goods." - Aristotle[265]

"'Come, Mr. Frodo!' he cried. 'I can't carry it for you, but I can carry you and it as well. So up you get!'[266] – Samwise Gamgee in Tolkien's *The Lord of the Rings*[267]

"To the Ancients, Friendship seemed the happiest and most fully human of all loves; the crown of life and the school of virtue. The modern world, in comparison, ignores it."
– C. S. Lewis[268]

"All kinds of things rejoiced my soul in their company – to talk and laugh and do each other kindness; read pleasant books together, pass from lightest jesting to talk of the deepest things and back again; differ without rancour, as a man might differ with himself, and when most rarely dissension arose, find our normal agreement all the sweeter for it; teach each other or learn from each other; be impatient for the return of the absent, and welcome them with joy on their homecoming; these and such like things,

---

[265] Aristotle, *Nicomachean Ethics*, 2nd edition, trans. Terence Irwin (Indianapolis, IN: Hackett Publishing Company1999), 119. VIII.1.5.
[266] J. R. R. Tolkien, *The Lord of the Rings* (NY: Houghton Mifflin Company, 1994), 919.
[267] I have a painting of this scene in my library. It is one of my favorite moments in which the saving power of burden-bearing friendship is on display! I am grateful for the 'Sam's in my life and am certain I would have stumbled short of my purpose had not God in his grace given them to me.
[268] C. S. Lewis, *The Four Loves* (NY: Harcourt Books, 1988), 57.

proceeding from our hearts as we gave affection and received it back, and shown by face, by voice, by the eyes, and a thousand other pleasant ways, kindled a flame which fused our very souls and of many made us one." – St. Augustine[269]

Questions for Further Reflection:

1. In what other ways does Jesus model true friendship?

2. Does 2 Corinthians 6:14 apply to friendships between a believer and an unbeliever?

3. Jesus was criticized for being a "friend of sinners" (see Matthew 11:19). How does this relate to cautions against friendship with wicked people (see 1 Corinthians 15:33)?

---

[269] Augustine, *Confessions*, 62-62. 4.VIII.13.

10. DAVID, BATHSHEBA, NATHAN, & ME
or CONVICTION, REPENTANCE, AND GRACE
or HOW TO RECEIVE GOD'S WORD

"For the word of God is living and active,

sharper than any two-edged sword,

piercing to the division of soul and of spirit,

of joints and marrow,

and discerning the thoughts and intentions of the heart.

And no creation is hidden…"

- Hebrews 4:12-13

As we look at a famous episode in David's life we see a story and a model of conviction, repentance, and grace through all of it. I want us to be reminded that what is wrong with the world is sin and apart from Jesus we are all sinners. Scripture shows us that the world is that it is full of wrongdoers. As wrongdoers we need to repent and fling ourselves upon the mercy and grace of God.

Pray & Read: 2 Samuel 11:1-12:15; Psalm 51

1. What stands out to you in this story?

2. Think about your reaction to Nathan's story in chapter 12. Was it similar to David's reaction? Did you feel frustration, anger, or disgust? What was your reaction to chapter 11? Similar? Even stronger?

3. Think of a sin you have recently committed. What was your reaction? Do you hear God's word saying "You are the man!" as you react to chapter 11? Why or why not?

4. From the text, what do we see as appropriate responses to God's word exposing our sin and rebellion?

5. How does this passage testify to Christ?

6. What does this passage mean for you as one who is *in Christ?*

7. What are you going to do in response? Who can you get to help you?

FOR FURTHER STUDY

Something to Read

Let's do some summary and background work for what happens in 2 Samuel 12.

By this point David is king. It was a long time coming and he went through a lot to get there, but he is seeing the fulfillment of God's promise and is now king.

If you were reading your Bible chronologically, and did not know how it ends, you could think that David looks like a decent option as the fulfillment of God's promise to provide a Savior king who would make things right in the whole world. Davis is a king and is wildly successful. He has taken down Goliath and many armies that were a threat to God's people.[270] The reach of the kingdom of Israel has gotten bigger and richer under his reign than it has ever been before.

God then makes some more promises that we find in 2 Samuel 7. God tells David that he will have "a great name, like the name of the great ones of the earth."[271] He also promises to establish a Kingdom through a son who would come from him. In this Kingdom, there would be peace and rest and violent men will not afflict or disturb anyone anymore. It will be a kingdom that will last forever. So it becomes clear that David is not the promised one that we have been looking for since Genesis 3:15, but there are still some pretty great things going on here and we now know that it will be a son of David!

---

[270] 1 Samuel 17, 30, 2 Samuel 5, 8, 10.
[271] 2 Samuel 7:9.

So David prays, saying "And now, O LORD GOD, you are God, and your words are true, and you have promised this good thing to your servant."[272] And the next few chapters show David living in the truth of God's promises.

He is having victories over enemies that are seeking to destroy them.[273] There are stories of him being kind to unexpected people and basically being a really awesome king. It's summed up in 2 Samuel 8:15, "So David reigned over all Israel. And David administered justice and equity to all his people."

Then we get to the story of David and Bathsheba.

It is a well-known story. I remember as a child seeing one of those planes at the beach that pulls a banner behind it with a message. It says on it something like, "Tonight at 8: David & Bathsheba." Remarkably, this is a story that David tries to cover up and here is a banner on the back of a plane at the beach three thousand years later talking about the story.

Movies have been made about this story. Books have been written. One of the Sherlock Holmes books follows the plot of David and Bathsheba.[274] Songs have been written about it. There's a song "Hallelujah" written by Leonard Cohen in 1985 that is about this story that has been so popular that it's been covered enough times for Newsweek to rank the top 60 covers of the song![275] It's been on American Idol and X-Factor and there is a BBC documentary about it and it is a part

---

[272] 2 Samuel 7:28.
[273] This is good for us since the promised Savior of the world was coming though Judah. By preserving David, he is preserving his plan to bring Jesus into the world.
[274] *The Adventure of the Crooked Man*
[275] http://www.newsweek.com/60-versions-leonard-cohens-hallelujah-ranked–303580

of the soundtrack for the movie "Shrek."[276] A song on the soundtrack for Shrek! About this story! My point is, it's a pretty well-known story.

David's abuse of his position and authority to take a woman that is not his wife is certainly adultery, but could very well amount to rape.[277] Then he has her husband killed as a part of the cover-up. These are two offenses that deserve the death penalty.[278] God had made it clear what punishment David deserves. David did an awful thing and he thought that he was powerful enough, protected enough, to get away with it. He, just like Adam and Eve and every other person before him, thought that he could hide from the consequences of his sin.

Then we get to 2 Samuel 12. Read (again) 2 Samuel 12:1-7.

David is confronted by the word of God through the prophet Nathan. David 'hears' the word, but misses the point when he fails to make the connection to his own sin. David rightly condemns the unjust man of Nathan's story. His 'moral compass,' his conscience, is intact and working. The innate understanding that

---

[276] "The Fourth, the Fifth, the Minor Fall"
[277] Scripture does not tell us if Bathsheba was a consenting participant in the sin. However, David's position of power and authority over Bathsheba, makes it impossible for an observer of the events to know whether she consented or not. Given her circumstances, even an admission of consent would be an unreliable indicator of her desire since she could have been seeking to protect herself by submitting to the demands of the king. It is not uncommon for sexual abuse victims to recognize something familiar in Bathsheba's circumstances.
[278] Adultery/Rape: Lev. 20:10; Deut. 22:25. Murder: Gen. 9:6; Lev. 24:17-23; Num. 35:9-34. You can also add in false witness to a capital crime as a third offense: Deut. 19:15-21.

God demands justice is present, but he is suppressing it when it comes to himself.[279]

He sees injustice and sin as wrong and deserving of punishment. He is angry and wants to see the wrong be made right, without seeing that he has been in the wrong and that he is deserving of a just punishment from God.

Incredibly, when we read this story about David, we often do exactly what David did when he heard Nathan's story. When we hear this story of David we think that he is so bad and so wrong, and, well, he is. We see him as beneath us and worse than us. We see him ignore what is obvious and scoff at him in our hearts. We turn our noses up at him because he doesn't recognize that the story is plainly about him.

And when we think these thoughts and believe these things in our heart. When we condemn David for his sin and declare that he deserves to die, the word of God speaks. That word which is like a two-edged sword. So sharp, so very sharp.[280] That word which discerns the thoughts and intentions of the heart. The word that exposes all cuts to our heart saying "You are the man!"

You are the one!

I am the one!

I am the sinner!

You are the sinner!

We become exactly like David when we condemn him. When we read this story and see ourselves more like

---

[279] Not surprising if we remember Romans 1:18.
[280] Hebrews 5:12–13.

Nathan than David, that is when we are most like David.

All of Scripture, every page of it, points us to Jesus. This is one of those sections that show us just how sinful man is and how deserving of death we are. David is not the promised son of God who will deliver us. David had major sin in his life. So it is with us. Scripture is showing us that we are the ones who deserve death. We are the ones who have rejected the One who is Good, True, Beautiful, and Life-giving. We rejected him and have found the only alternative: that which is bad, false, ugly, and leads to death.

Don't miss it! Scripture convicts sinners of sin. It shows wrongdoers that they do wrong. It shows each and every one of us that we not only suffer wrong, but that we all also commit wrong. We have, at different times, been the Uriah's and Bathsheba's as victims of the story. We may at times share God's word as the Nathan's of the story. But we must not lose sight of the fact that we have all been the David's of the story.

We are like David, but there is an opportunity for things to be made right.

We can repent. We can turn from our sin. We can be people who are made from wrongdoers into right-doers. There is a forgiveness, a grace, a gift, a promise, and an underserved-making-of-things-right that comes in believing that God has provided One who can save us.

David already knew that God had promised a son would come. We know that a son who is the Savior is the one who would eventually come and save, not only from the death that is deserved, but also from the hold and cycle of sin and darkness. So David throws himself at the mercy of God. Knowing that he deserves death, he cries out:

(Re)Read Psalm 51.

And God doesn't kill him. David does not receive the execution he deserves. There are consequences to his actions, but the Lord shows him grace. He shows him mercy.[281]

You know why? Because God has made promises and God keeps His promises.[282] Those promises relate to salvation for you, me, and David.

"God so loved the world that he [would] give his only Son, that whoever believes in him should not perish but have eternal life."[283]

God had a plan to save sinners and create in them a new heart. A plan that involved a son of David. One born in the line of Abraham, Isaac, and Jacob. One who is the Lion of Judah.[284] One who is prophet, priest, and King. One who has been face to face with the Father.[285] One who was not only the son of David, but the root of David.[286] One who is the source of life. One who would die the death that we were supposed to die and then be resurrected to offer us life if we will repent and turn from our wrongdoing and trust and follow him. He is Jesus. He is the Christ. He is the promised one. He is the one that will make things right.

---

[281] It was pointed out to me that this is one of the most controversial parts of this story. Wrestle with it! It is good for us to wonder why God would do this. Was he caught off guard by David's actions, but on the hook to still fulfill his promises? Why let some sinners off and punish others? Keep reading and if you are not satisfied by the answers coming up, continue to pray, ask the Lord about it, and talk to other believers to work it out.
[282] Remember 2 Sam. 7:12-14 especially.
[283] John 3:16.
[284] Compare Gen. 49:9-10 and Rev. 5:5.
[285] Compare Deut. 18:15 and John 1:18.
[286] Rev. 5:5.

David looked forward to the Messiah's coming even as he had an extremely limited knowledge of what that meant. David did not know that his name would be Jesus, and understood very little about what to expect, but he did know that he could put his trust in the promises of God that the Lord would establish an everlasting throne through his line. David did not know that his deliver was the Christ and he did not know that the Christ's name would be Jesus,[287] but he still looked forward in faith, trusting in God's faithfulness to fulfill his promises.

We know that His name is Jesus. The grace that was there for David is here for us today. Believe God's promise to make things right through Jesus.

Turn from sin and believe the promise that Jesus can and will create in you a new heart and take you into His Kingdom that will last forever.

Psalm 51 is a powerful word for us. In it we have the words of a man who realizes his sin and is trusting God's grace and mercy to deliver him.

If you are reading this and realize that you don't know Jesus, hear the words of Scripture showing you that you are a sinner. You are the wrongdoer in the story. You are the man! Scripture shows you that you are like David in his sin, you deserve death. But Scripture also shows us that you can be like David in his repentance.

---

[287] Remember the textual and epochal context that we previously discussed. David is still about a thousand years away from the coming of Jesus. There is a whole lot more in the Old Testament to be revealed about God's plan for redemption through his Servant, but David would have known some things. By believing in the promises God gave him, he was participating in the same faith that we share. We experience it with a much greater clarity that comes from living in our epoch since we have the whole canonical context to understand what was going on in 2 Samuel 11-12 and Psalm 51.

Repent, turn from sin, and trust Jesus to make things right in your heart.

If you know Jesus, and have been following Him, know that Jesus is at work making things right in your heart. Even now. One of the ways he does this is by showing us the sin in our lives that we still hold onto. Take time to consider what the Lord might be showing you. Perhaps a habit of sin that you cannot seem to break. Perhaps it is a short temper. Maybe it's a readiness to gossip and talk about others. Maybe it is a giving in to pornography or a failure to do what you know you need to do. It could be a failure to prioritize God in your time or in your friendships. Maybe it is a failure to try to be a good student or a good son or a good daughter. A failure "to do everything for the glory of God."[288] Maybe it is something else.

Whatever it is, confess that sin. Repent. And trust the work of Christ.

Thank him that he has already begun in your life the work described in Psalm 51.

Some Related Scripture Passages:

Proverbs 2:1-5

Romans 7:18-8:17

Romans 10:9-13

Hebrews 6

---

[288] Colossians 3:17.

James 1:22-27

1 John 1:5-10

Questions for Further Reflection:

1. Is it fair that David did not face the death penalty for his sins? Shouldn't that have been a part of the consequences of his sin? How is God just for letting him get off so easy?

2. Isn't it unfair that the baby that was conceived by David and Bathsheba died?[289] How do you square that with God letting David live?

3. What specific things does David ask of God in Psalm 51? For example: "have mercy," "wash me," "purge me."

4. What specific things does David say will happen in response to the Lord granting his plea for mercy?

5. In Psalm 51:10 David pleaded for God to give him a "clean heart." Did God answer that prayer? Have you been given a clean heart? How do you know?

---

[289] 2 Sam. 12:14-18.

11. GOD'S WILL FOR YOUR LIFE
or HOW TO GO FROM HERE

"Then Gideon said to God,

'Let not your anger burn against me;

let me speak just once more.

Please LET ME TEST just once more with the fleece.

Please let it be dry on the fleece only, and on all the ground

let there be dew.'

AND GOD DID SO that night;

and it was dry on the fleece only, and on all the ground

there was dew."

Judges 6:39-40[290]

What does next week look like for you? How about next month? The next year? Where will you be in five years?

It is a common Christian concern want to know how to discern the Lord's will. It seems to be largely born out of a desire to serve him faithfully and fulfill what he has called us to in life. Sometimes, there are less holy motivations as well: fear of failure, a leaning towards

---

[290] It is important to ask if a passage of Scripture is prescriptive (telling us what to do) or descriptive (recounting what happened). Not every example is offered for us to follow. Does the Bible hold up Gideon's actions as worth emulation?

worry and anxiety, and a desire to easily follow the path of your life.

The answer to knowing God's will for your life - and how you should go from here - is both simpler and more challenging than we typically think.

Pray & Read: James 1:5; Proverbs 3:5-6; Isaiah 48:17

1. What stands out to you from these passages?

2. According to these passages, what does God require of you?

3. According to these passages, what does God promise to do for you?

4. How do you want God to show you his leading? Does God promise to show you in that way? If so, excellent! If not, how do you change your expectations to match his promises?

5. How does this passage testify to Christ?

6. What does this passage mean for you as one who is *in Christ*?

7. What are you going to do in response? Who can you get to help you?

FOR FURTHER STUDY

Something to Read

You may be at a time in your life when you are facing a lot of questions about your future. You can feel the pressure of upcoming decisions and a desire to get them right so you do not screw up your life! As a believer, you are likely concerned about following God's will for your life. It is your desire to live the life he has called you to and so you want to be careful to make good, God-honoring decisions. You want to walk in wisdom. It is possible you feel like the next few years will be pivotal for your life, and they might be. I am not sure that any of the years you will face won't eventually be seen as pivotal in some way or another. The journey to understand the direction one's life will take is an old and familiar quest. Unsurprisingly, Scripture is not silent on the issue. God has not left us to wander aimlessly nor has he placed us in a position where we have to grope in the darkness after his plans for our lives.

Before we go too far, we should acknowledge that there is another question that man has wrestled with since ancient times: are we fated or free? Has my life been planned for me or do I choose my own destiny? Scripture addresses this question in two ways. First, the Bible speaks as though God is in sovereign control of all things.[291] He is the creator and the almighty God that rules over all. Second, the Bible speaks as through man is responsible for his own actions.[292] Both truths are presented in Scripture and we may want to push back a little bit on these truths and ask for an

---

[291] Psalm 139:16; Isaiah 37:26; Ephesians 1:3-10.
[292] Joshua 24:15; Matthew 16:28. Additionally, any command in the Bible implies a decision to either obey or reject that command.

explanation of how both claims can be true, but Scripture does not spell that out for us. However, we can see it at work in the Bible.

Consider the example of Jonah. God issues a command to the prophet Jonah to go preach to the terrifyingly wicked people of Nineveh.[293] Jonah flees in the opposite direction as he takes a ship towards Tarshish instead and God sends a storm. Jonah confesses to his fellow frightened travelers that his rebellion is the cause of the storm, but rather than repent and ask that they return towards Nineveh, Jonah continues in his rebellion as he decides he would rather be thrown over board to drown in the sea than obey God's command.[294] Instead of drowning, he is swallowed by a great fish from whose belly he prays to the LORD and three days later he is spewed onto dry land.[295] Jonah then proceeds to begrudgingly preach to the people of Nineveh and they repent and are spared.

There is often a lot of unfortunate talk around this story about the will of God. Some people will say that Jonah was outside of God's will when he fled God's command and I get the desire to say that; Jonah was definitely rebellious. But in what sense is God in control of all things if anything can be outside of his will? Others like to talk about God's permissive will or speak as though God has a perfect plan, but some sort of alternate less-good plan. In the example of Jonah, going to Nineveh right of way would have been God's

---

[293] Jonah 1:1.
[294] Jonah 1:12.
[295] Some people see this story as so fantastical that it cannot be literally true. However, I do not see a need to understand it as a metaphor. If I can believe that Jesus was crucified, buried, resurrected three days later, ascended to heaven, and will one day return in the sky riding on a white horse to judge the living and the dead, I can believe that a fish swallowed a man who happened to then survive the experience.

perfect plan for Jonah, but going via the whale was a part of God's permissive plan. Or, some might say, Jonah was outside of God's will on the ship but God used the fish to bring him back into his plan.

Ultimately, I find this kind of language unhelpful. God having a permissive plan does not really alleviate the problem some people have of man not getting any meaningful say in the manner. Whether you are in God's perfect will or his permissive will are you not still just doing what he wants and not what you want? It is like being offered green beans or peas for every meal of your life and proudly exclaiming that you get to eat whatever you want.

Furthermore, things get more complicated when we remember that the New Testament informs us that Jonah's time in the fish, which was a consequence of his rebellion to God's command, is an act that prophesies the death, burial, and resurrection of Jesus.[296] In what way can Jonah's rebellion be outside of God's will if it was a means of prophesying the coming Christ?[297] There has to be a way in which it was all a part of God's plan, however we also see that God holds Jonah responsible for his actions in the story. The example of the story of Jonah reminds us that we need to be careful about the statements we make when we speak about God's will.

We see another example of God's sovereign will and man's responsibly at work in the crucifixion of Jesus. Who killed the Christ? Was it sovereign God or wicked men? Was it God's plan or man's plan? Peter tells us in his Pentecost sermon that Jesus was "delivered up by the definite plan and foreknowledge of God" and that

---

[296] Matthew 16:4; 1 Corinthians 15:4.
[297] It is arguable *the only* Old Testament passage that prophesies a burial of three days and then a resurrection.

he was "killed by the hands of lawless man."[298] In the crucifixion of Jesus we see that the most evil, rebellious act against God man has ever committed – the murder of God – is also the most gracious act that God has ever committed towards man – the provision of our salvation through the self-sacrifice of Jesus. Man is fully responsible, but we also see that it was all according to God's plan. Scripture does not explain exactly how this could be so, but lets us know that it is.[299]

Let these two examples affirm that we should both care about obedience and following God's plan and trust that God is in control. With that in mind, we can consider how you can know what God's plan is for your life. It is right for us to care about God's will. Jesus modeled that for us in his prayers: "Your kingdom come, your will be done" and "nevertheless, not my will, but yours, be done."[300] And James admonishes believers to not to brazenly boast about plans about tomorrow but to instead say, "If the Lord wills, we will live and do this or do that."[301]

Here is the big moment and the big reveal of how to know God's will for your life:

GOD'S PLAN FOR YOUR LIFE IS REVEALED IN HIS WORD.

---

[298] Acts 2:23.
[299] Theologians have offered a variety of explanations of how God can be in control and man also be responsible for his own actions. While there is not widespread agreement on what system of explanation, they generally affirm the two truths that God is in control and man is responsible/accountable for his actions. To learn more about possible explanations offered over the years, review: Calvinism, Molinism, Amyraldism, Pelagianism, Arminianism, Pelagianism, and Semi-Pelagianism.
[300] Matthew 6:10; Luke 22:42.
[301] James 4:13-15.

As before, I use 'his Word' in a deliberately ambiguous manner. We know, as we have seen, that our life finds meaning, purpose, fulfillment, and direction in the one who is the Word: Jesus. God's plan, also know as his will, for us is to be like Jesus.[302] We also know, and have seen, that Jesus is revealed through the word of God: the Bible. So we turn to our Bibles to see Jesus and understand God's vision and planned shape for our lives.[303] We are to live and be like him.

Now you may be disregarding this explanation saying, "I know, I know, that God wants us to be like Jesus, but that is not what I meant. I want to know where to go to college, what major to choose, whom to marry, where to live, where to work, how many kids to have, when to retire, and whether or not I should green beans or peas with my next meal." But those are not the answers God gives us and we cannot be in a position of faithful trust in the Lord's control and demand that he give us answers that we deem more important or useful than what he has given us in his Word.

God has reveled through his word that if we focus on obedience in what he has revealed of his will through his, then we can trust that God is guiding our steps and making our paths straight. Think about Proverbs 3:5-6, "Trust in the LORD with all your heart, and do not lean on your understanding. In all your ways acknowledge him, and he will make straight your paths." God's will is that you trust him and walk. Do not wait for him to tell you when to turn to the left or

---

[302] Romans 8:28-29.

[303] I make an effort to avoid saying, "I believe the Lord's will is _____" unless the "_____" is something from Scripture. Scripture is where God has chosen to reveal his will and desires, so how else could we rightly speak about his will apart from Scripture?

the right; just trust and walk and he will make the path straight.

If you want to know what college to go to, trust God as you obey his revealed will that you love him with all your heart, soul, and mind and love your neighbor as yourself and you will end up in the right place.[304] If you want to know who to date or marry or where to work, obey God in sanctification as you abstain from sexual immorality and show brotherly love, for this is the will of God, and you can trust that God will straighten out those other things.[305] The New Testament epistles are full of explanations of what it looks like to live in Christ and so fulfill the will of God. It becomes evident that God is much less concerned about where you go to school or work than he is about what kind of person you are *in Jesus* in those places.

All that being said, you will still have to make decisions in life and you will want to get them right. Knowing that God is guiding your steps should relieve you of worry and anxiety regarding those decisions. It should give you a sense of freedom to live and act as a child of God, but such living is not without care or discernment. So here are seven steps for making good decisions:

1. Pray that God would guide your steps and make you sensitive to his Spirit's leading.

God has promised that his Spirit will guide us and he has promised to give us wisdom if we ask for it.[306] When we pray in such a way, we are praying in a way that he has asked us to pray and with a request that he has promised to answer.

---

[304] Matthew 22:37
[305] 1 Thessalonians 4:3-12.
[306] Proverbs 3:5-6; Isaiah 48:17; John 16:13.

2. Read your Bible and learn about how God wants you to live on a day-to-day basis.

Make this a habit. God has revealed so much about what life in Christ looks like. Peter tells us that Jesus has already walked in the path we should go and now we must follow in his steps.[307] His example is like the worksheet you use when you are first learning how to write your letters of the alphabet. As we read Scripture and learn more about Jesus we are tracing the pattern that he has laid out for us that we might become familiar with what it looks like to live like him. The more we follow his lead the more familiar the motions become.

3. Use the reason and wisdom God has given you.

When you are making a decision, make sure you are considering all of your options. Evaluate those options to determine if one makes more sense than the other. Perhaps one provides more opportunities to advance the kingdom of Christ or will allow you to more clearly fulfill the commands that God has revealed in Scripture. You will be able to easily eliminate any option that is wicked or rebellious towards God, but sometimes you will realize that all of the options seem like good options. It could be the case that all options could equally allow for you to grow in sanctification and service of the Lord. There may be no clear frontrunner at this point and that it is okay, but make sure that you have carefully considered what all of your options actually are.

---

[307] 1 Peter 2:21.

4. Consider what you want to do.[308]

God gives us desires and dreams and it is reasonable that they would play into the discernment process. We should be aware of those desires and evaluate if any of the options in our decision are better aligned with those dreams. It is important to note that not everything in life that you are supposed to do is going to feel like something that you have always wanted to do. One of the gifts that God gives his children is contentment in any circumstance.[309] So what we want cannot be the only factor in determining what is the right decision to make. We know that we can be content in any circumstance in obedience to God.[310] In fact, if we consider Jonah again, we know that God sometimes calls people to do things that they might be reluctant to do. It is important that we are in constant prayer and asking the Lord to break us of our sin as he conforms us more and more into the image of Jesus.

---

[308] Some would add to that you should consider what you are good at or where your giftings lie. However, in Scripture, gifts and talents are given to serve the Lord and serve the people of God. So it is a worthwhile consideration, but it often gets misapplied to determining a career or a calling. Scripture does not use such discussions about your gifts and talents to point you to a career, but to how you can serve God and the church. Those may align, but it should not be assumed that it will be so. Furthermore, God often takes people that are weak in a particular area to use them in their weakness. So using what you are talented in as an indicator for what sort of decision you should make should be used very carefully and with these cautions in mind.

[309] Philippians 4:11-13.

[310] This is the point of Philippians 4:13.

5. Consult other Christians.

God often uses others to speak truth to us. It is good for us to have friends that know us and can help us discern what is right in a decision. God has gifted other believers with wisdom and discernment and it may be that he wants to use his Spirit in them to bear the burden of your decision with you. There is a unification that occurs when believers share their lives with one another, so it should not come as a surprise that the Lord often chooses to speak through other people to us.

6. Make a decision.

Just do it. You do not want to be stuck in indecision. If you have worked through the above list and still have not determined what you should do, flip a quarter. Then if you realize while it is in the air that you hope it lands a certain way, just do that thing that you hoped for. Otherwise, let the quarter decide.

7. Act and move forward in faith.

When I find myself making a significant decision I try to pray something like this:

> Lord, this seems to be the best thing to do. I have prayed about it, thought about it, and sought to discern what is the right thing to do. This seems best to me. If it is not what you want, then you are going to have to make it clear to me or do something to prevent me from walking down this path, otherwise I am moving forward.

147

I do not see such a prayer as testing God, but rather as a step of faith trusting that God is faithful to his promises to keep his children and guide their steps. We make a decision and move forward. If we have misread the situation, the Lord is capable of guiding us and that is exactly what he has promised to do. It is not the timid testing of Gideon, but the kind of obedient decision-making prayerful action of Christ in the garden of Gethsemane. So be free! Move forward and act as though you are a child of God because you are!

Some Related Scripture Passages:

Genesis 50:20

Psalm 139:16

Matthew 11:28

John 15:16

1 Corinthians 1:6-16

Ephesians 2:8-10

James 4:13-17

1 Peter 2:13-25

Revelation 4:11

Some Quotes:

"God's will in this age is that his people be scattered like salt and light in all legitimate vocations. His aim is to be known, because knowing him is life and joy. He does not call us out of the world. He does not remove the need to work. He does not destroy society and culture. Through his scattered saints he spreads a passion for his supremacy in all things for the joy of all peoples. If you work like the world, you will waste your life, no matter how rich you get. But if your work creates a web of redemptive relationships and becomes an adornment for the Gospel of the glory of Christ, your satisfaction will last forever and God will be exalted in your joy."

- John Piper[311]

"Success is not determined by what I accomplish, but rather by my faithfulness – faithfulness to the One who called me and to his gracious invitation."

- Jamin Goggin[312]

Questions for Further Reflection:

1. Are you satisfied with my explanation of how to know God's will for your life? Why or why not?

2. Do you accept that God is in control of all things? If so, why does he hold us accountable for what we have done? If not, how can we be certain that he will accomplish what he has promised to accomplish?

---

[311] John Piper, *Don't Waste Your Life* (Wheaton, IL: Crossway Books, 2003), 154.
[312] Jim Goggin and Kyle Strobel, *The Way of the Dragon or the Way of the Lamb* (Nashville, TN: Nelson Books, 2017), 129.

3. Do you accept that man is responsible for his own actions? If so, in what sense is God responsible for what is happening in the world? If not, is man in any sense free?

4. How should you understand bad decisions that you have made in your life?

BIBLIOGRAPHY

Anselm. *Cur Deus Homo.* available at https://www.
    ewtn.com/library/CHRIST/CURDEUS.HTM.
————. *Proslogion.* available at https://sourcebooks.
    fordham.edu/basis/anselm- proslogium.asp.

Aristotle. trans. Hugh Lawson-Tancred. *Metaphysics.* NY:
    Penguin Books, 1998.
————. trans. Terence Irwin. *Nicomachean Ethics*, 2nd edition.
    Indianapolis, IN: Hackett Publishing Company, 1999.

Augustine. trans. F. J. Sheed. *Confessions.* Indianapolis, IN:
    Hackett Publishing, 2006.
————. trans. John Gibb and James Innes, ed. Philip Schaff .
    "Tractate XXIX" in *Nicene and Post-Nicene Fathers:*
    Augustin – Gospel of John, First Epistle of John,
    Soliloquies, vol 7. Peabody, MA: Hendrickson
    Publishers, 2012.

Aurelius, Marcus. *Meditations.* NY: Penguin Books, 2005.

Berry, Wendell. *Sex, Economy, Freedom & Community.* .NY:
    Pantheon Books, 1993.

Carroll, B. H. *Inspiration of the Bible.* Nashville: Thomas
    Nelson, 1980.

Chesterton, G. K. *The Everlasting Man.* San Francisco, CA:
    Ignatius Press, 1993.

Childs, Brevard S. *Biblical Theology of the Old and New*
    Testaments: Theological Reflection on the Christian Bible.
    Minneapolis, MN: Fortress Press, 2011.

Chrysostom, John. trans. W. R. W. Stephens, ed. Philip
    Schaff. "Against Marcionsists and Manicheans, on
    the Passage 'Father, If it be Possible,'" in *Nicene &*

Post-Nicene Fathers: Chrysostom – On the Priesthood, Ascetic Treatises, Select Homilies and Letters, Homilies on the Statutes, vol. 9. Peabody, MA: Hendrickson Publishers, 2012.

Dawkins, Richard. *The God Delusion.* NY: Houghton Mifflin Company, 2006.

Dostoevsky, Fyodor. *The Brothers Karamazov,* trans. Constance Garnett. NY: Barnes & Noble Classics, 2004.

Ehrman, Bart D. *Lost Christianities: The Battles for Scripture and the Faiths We Never Knew.* NY: Oxford University Press, 2003.

Greear, J. D. *Gospel: Recovering the Power that Made Christianity Revolutionary.* Nashville, TN: B&H Publishing Group, 2011.

Goggin, Jim and Kyle Strobel. *The Way of the Dragon or the Way of the Lamb.* Nashville, TN: Nelson Books, 2017.

Goldsworthy, Graeme. *According to Plan: The Unfolding Revelation of God in the Bible.* Downers Grove, IL: InterVarsity Press, 2002.
———. *Gospel-Centered Hermeneutics: Foundations and Principles of Evangelical Biblical Interpretation.* Downers Grove, IL: InterVarsity Press, 2006.

Gutiérrez, Gustavo. *The Power of the Poor in History.* Maryknoll, NY : Orbis Books, 1983.

Hunter, Trent & Stephen Wellum. *Christ from Beginning to End: How the Full Story of Scripture Reveals the Full Glory of Christ.* Grand Rapids, MI: Zondervan, 2018.

Lewis, C. S. "First and Second Things" in *The Collected Works of C. S. Lewis.* NY: Inspirational Press, 1996.
———. *The Four Loves* NY: Harcourt Books, 1988.
———. *The Last Battle.* NY: HarperTrophy, 2000.
———. *Miracles.* NY: HarperCollinsPublishers, 1996.

Lints, Richard. *The Fabric of Theology: A Prolegomenon to Evangelical Theology*. Grand Rapids, Mich: Eerdmans, 1993.

Milton, John. *Paradise Lost.* NY: Penguin Books, 2000.

Moore, Russel D. "Beyond a Veggie Tales Gospel: Why We Must Preach Christ From Every Text" accessed at https://www.russellmoore.com/2008/05/19/beyond-a-veggie-tales- gospel-why-we-must-preach-christ-from-every-text/ on March 16, 2019.
———. *Onward: Engaging the Culture Without Losing the Gospel.* Nashville, TN: B&H Publishing Group, 2015.
———.*Tempted and Tried*. Wheaton, IL: Crossway, 2011.

O'Connor, Flannery. *The Complete Stories.* NY: Farrar, Straus and Giroux, 1971.

Packer, J. I. "Good Question: Text Criticism and Inerrancy" in *Christianity Today.* October 7, 2002.

Piper, John. *Don't Waste Your Life*. Wheaton, IL: Crossway Books, 2003.

Plato. trans. G. M. A. Grube, ed. John M. Cooper. *Plato: Complete Works*. Indianapolis, IN: Hackett Publishing Company, 1997.

Schreiner, Thomas R. *The King in His Beauty: A Biblical Theology of the Old and New Testaments.* Grand Rapids, MI: Baker Academic, 2013.

Tolkien, J. R. R. *The Lord of the Rings*. NY: Houghton Mifflin Company, 1994.

Voltaire. trans. Henry Morley. *Candide.* NY: Barnes & Noble Classics, 2003.

Walvoord, John F. and Roy B. Zuck, eds. *The Bible Knowledge Commentary: New Testament*. Colorado Springs, CO: Victor, 2000.

Wilson, Jared C. *Gospel Deeps.* Wheaton, IL: Crossway 2012.